HHP

"Vinyl, vinyl, read all about it!"

Copyright © 2019 Randy McNutt

ISBN: 978-1-7321838-5-8

Published by HHP Books, an imprint of the Hamilton Hobby Press, Inc.

Vintage Tape Recorders is in HHP Books' Classic Vinyl Collector Series.

Vintage Tape Recorders

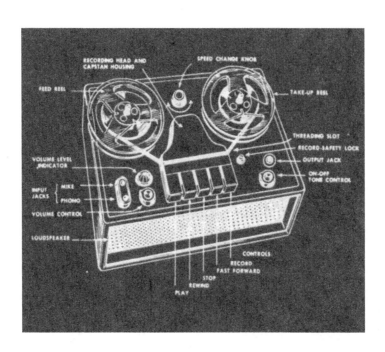

A 3M Recorder, 1958.

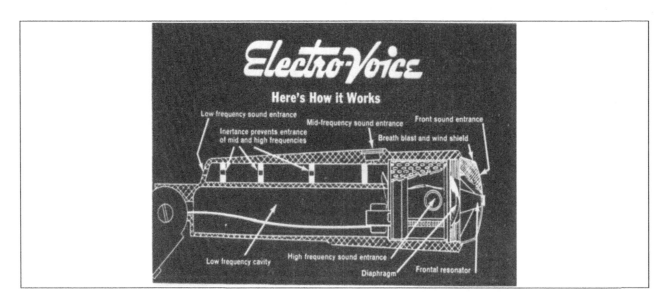

May 1957: Electro-Voice brings you its high fidelity 664, which the company says brings no "boominess" from close voices. The mic's "exclusive, indestructible Acoustalloy diaphragm—a single moving element," can withstand mechanical shocks and heat. I intended for hi-fi and professional jobs.

Vintage Tape Recorders

*A Pictorial History of Professional Tape Machines,
Forgotten Recording Studios, and Assorted Gear*

Randy McNutt

HHP BOOKS
Hamilton, Ohio

Praise for HHP Books' Classic Vinyl Collector Series

We Wanna Boogie: An Illustrated History of the American Rockabilly Movement

"It is an extensive oral history, featuring commentaries from a broad spectrum or rockabilly artists—famous and unknown—and influential record company executives of the fifties. The vintage photographs that the author presents in *We Wanna Boogie* are marvelous and capture the uncomplicated vitality of early rockabilly performers . . . *Boogie* is a carefully compiled, beautifully illustrated introduction to the rockabilly scene at the dawn of the rock era   . . . This study is a superb supplement to earlier works by Nick Tosches, Peter Guralnick, Bob Garbutt, and Adam Komorowski."

B. Lee Cooper
Popular Music and Society

Too Hot to Handle: An Illustrated Encyclopedia of American Recording Studios of the 20th Century

"This 223-page book is exactly what its name implies, a listing of many of the most important studios in America from Edison to the turn of the century. Randy has searched out many of the old studios while traveling and he has talked to a good number of engineers, musicians and studio owners about past studio locations. . . . If ever there was inspiration for me to keep my little studio alive this book is it."

Larry Crane
Tape Op

Spinning the Groove: An A to Z Guide to the Lingo and Legacy of the Old Record Business

"This is a must-have encyclopedic adventure for audiophiles, record collectors, social historians, and vinyl aficionados everywhere. It is packed with cool lingo, in-depth definitions and stories of the old record business, plus great recording history and stories of colorful characters, DJs, musicians, producers, and label owners. A great collection of old ads from the days when 45s were all the rage. No record collection will be complete without this book."

Alison James
"Million Dollar Hot Wax Weekends" WKRC Cincinnati

Available from Amazon.com and other booksellers.

Dedication

To Valdemar Poulsen,
inventor of the Telegraphon, the
first magnetic recorder, 1898,

and to Gene Lawson, left, recording engineer,
drummer, and creator of the Lawson Microphone.
Shown here with author Randy McNutt in 2016.

The Ampex 300 series wasn't the company's first pro recorders, but it was the one that introduced the tape sound to just about everyone in the business. Soon it would be a fixture in good recording studios, TV stations, and radio stations across the country. This is an early version, from 1949.

Contents

Arrival of the Magnetophone

J. Herbert Orr poses with the German Magnetophone he brought from Germany at the end of World War II. He had been a member of the Signal Corps that discovered the recorder that used plastic tape and ran it at 30 IPS. After the war, Orr settled in Opelika, Kansas, where he tinkered with tape recorders in the basement of a drug store. He founded the ORRadio company, a major manufacturer of recording tape.

THE TAPE RECORDER'S FIRST TEN YEARS: A BRIEF TIMELINE

1945: J. Herbert Orr brings a German-built Magnetophone—or Magnetophon—back back to the States from Germany at the end of World War II. He studies it and starts making recording tape. He is only one of a number of people who worked on perfecting the new tape recorder that the Germans had developed and used during the war.

1947: As 3M's company researchers develop a new magnetic material, making it possible to erase tape, the established wire recorder business hits a high point. It dominates the recording field. Seventeen companies make wire recorders. Only four are involved in making infant tape recorders—Brush, Amplifier Corporation of America, Reproducer Company, and Sound Recorder.

1948: Ampex Electric of California introduces its 200 model professional tape recorder—a breakthrough in recording music. Meanwhile, 3M starts selling red oxide recording tape. ABC buys twelve new Ampex recorders—they cost a whopping $5,200 each—and soon will buy a dozen more.

1949: Soon other manufacturers join Ampex. They include Fairchild, Magnecord, Presto, Ranger Tone, and RCA, and others would soon follow. Meanwhile, more companies enter the audio tape-manufacturing business, including Audio Devices. The company produces paper base tapes coated with black and red oxide.

1950: Twenty new recorder manufacturers turn out machines for fascinated public and business sectors. New firms include Allied Radio, Ampro, Concertone, Ekotape, Masco, Stancil-Hoffman, Webcor, and Wilcox-Gray. As the companies make recorders, J. Herbert Orr starts producing his Irish recording tape, made of a plastic base with oxide coating.

1951: Thanks to an enthralled public, tape recorders are the rage of the world. Obviously, wire recorders are fading.

1952: Tape recorders are still expensive by standards of the day. But "recordists," as operators of tape machines are called, want to buy.

1953: The Magnetic Recording Industry Association is formed by Joseph F. Hards to promote tape recording and help companies exchange suitable ideas. In September, RCA shows off its video tape recorder. But it would take two decades for it to become a hot item for consumers.

1954: Stereo recording gains momentum, particularly for home hi-fi fans. Magnecord continues its push into the professional and amateur markets, introducing its M-80, "a new high-quality machine" designed for recording studios and radio stations.

1955: The public's interest in tape recording does not lessen. Unfortunately, buyers are losing interest in wire recording. Tape clubs for both adults and teenagers pop up across the country and the world. Several magazines devote themselves to tape recording and promote "tape pals" to exchange home recordings.

1956: More companies enter the tape recorder business. Ampex retains its legendary status by improving its 300 series, the successor to the 200. One track is giving way to two.

1957: The number of recording studios increase in large cities and small towns. No longer do record label A&R men have to go to New York, Los Angeles, and Nashville to record at quality locations. Advances in recording technology offer two tracks, just as rock 'n' roll is beginning to boom. The race is on to the Top 40.

In 1950, Soundcraft produced tape and vinyl records.

WIRE RECORDERS! TABLE MODELS! CONSOLES!

Modern Table Radio
Silvertone Exclusive Styling

Reg. 34.95 **29⁹⁵**

Smooth finish walnut veneer cabinet with harmonizing grille cloth. Full toned 5¼-inch dynamic speaker.

Radio Phonograph

Reg. 105.00 NOW **89⁹⁵**

Silvertone quality in every feature! Thrill to the tones from the oval dynamic speaker. Automatic changer. Lustrous mahogany finish.

Wire Recorder

Reg. 169.50 NOW **129⁵⁰**

It's a radio, it's a phonograph, it's a WIRE RECORDER! Topflight entertainment for the whole family! See this sensation today!

Silvertone Portable

Reg. 39.95 NOW **32⁹⁵**

Trim and smart at a surprise low price! Plays clear and sweet on batteries, AC or DC. Ivory and gold colored metal; artificial trim.

When this ad appeared in 1950, the world was still obsessed with radio. Television hadn't yet invaded every niche of American life and geography. Vinyl records had only recently arrived, and wire and tape recorders were leading the way to a new strata of sound. The larger stores, including Sears, would help move the country into the new technologies. Through their efforts, the audio tape recorder would become popular for home use. But for audio professionals, much of the equipment found in recording studios, radio stations, and in television stations had to be custom-built or purchased from special dealers who specialized in selling equipment to the sound business. It would take decades before someone could enter a store and buy everything he needs to start a home recording studio that could rival some of the commercial ones in sound quality.

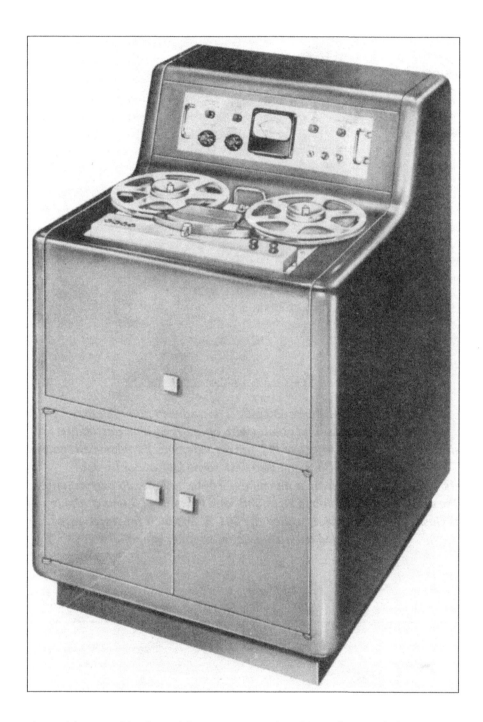

A washing machine? No, it's a Magnecord M-80 professional, from 1954.

The popular Ampex 600 model, introduced about 1954,
combined professional quality with home-recording portability.
Using a slower but still effective IPS, the recorder was popular with radio and
television stations and also with some low-budget record
producers who used the convenient machine to capture nightclub performances. Though
the original model weighed 28 pounds and was bulky, it was at the top of
its class. This 1958 version , called the 601-2, was built for stereo recording,
and needed a matched set of speaker-amplifiers.

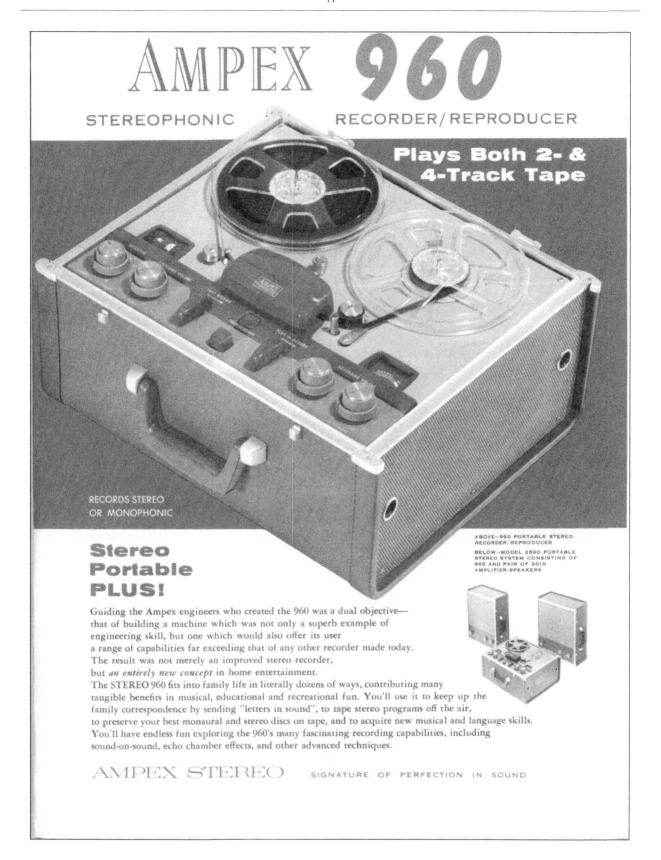

By Christmas of 1959, Ampex had a portable stereo recorder on the market. It was more user-friendly than the venerable 600 model. It looked more modern, too.

ONLY and ONLY V-M has "ADD-A-TRACK"

PLAY & RECORD /	SIDE ONE	SIDE TWO
	3	2
	1	4
PLAY /	ADD-A-TRACK	
	QUARTER TRACK STEREO	
	HALF TRACK STEREO	

THE **MOST** PRACTICAL, THE **MOST** USEABLE, THE **MOST** UNUSUAL FEATURE **ANY** TOP TAPE RECORDER HAS TO OFFER!

SEE-HEAR-COMPARE THE ALL-NEW V-M 'tape-o-matic'® FOUR-TRACK STEREO-PLAY TAPE RECORDER—MODEL 720

Amazing new "Add-A-Track" permits you to record on one track, add musical accompaniment or additional voices on the second track while listening to the first recording and on playback you hear both tracks simultaneously! This exclusive V-M feature has unlimited applications in education — in business — in industry, in addition to its appeal for pure "home entertainment"!

- PLAYS ALL STEREOPHONIC TAPES (2-track, 4-track either stacked or staggered)
- RECORDS AND PLAYS-BACK MONOPHONICALLY
- CATHOPTIC TUNING EYE FOR PROFESSIONAL-QUALITY RECORDING RESULTS
- HIGH-QUALITY, HIGH-FIDELITY MICROPHONE (included)
- BLUE-GRAY LEATHERETTE CASE — COMPLETELY PORTABLE   ONLY $225.00 list†
- MODEL 166 MATCHING AUXILIARY-AMPLIFIER SPEAKER COMPLETES YOUR STEREO SYSTEM $75.00 list†

†Slightly higher in the West

the Voice VM of Music®

V-M CORPORATION   BENTON HARBOR, MICHIGAN   WORLD FAMOUS FOR THE FINEST IN RECORD CHANGERS, PHONOGRAPHS AND TAPE RECORDERS

3

By 1959, the early and reliable Voice of Music company came out with an "add-a-track" feature, which must have made home recordists imagine they were on par with recording studios. This machine could serve as a field recorder or as a recorder for live performances.

Introduction

Ever since I received my first small reel-to-reel recorder for Christmas in 1962, I have enjoyed tape machines as sculptures as well as conduits of sound. Something fascinated me about the thin tape as it wound around small reels and moved smoothly through the heads. Though my junior-high school days have long passed, my fascination for magnetic recorders continues. Even in this day of digital recording, I still fumble around with two Tascam cassette recorders from the late 1980s. I also still produce records on tape—a twenty-four track Otari machine.

As a result of all this, *Vintage Tape Recorders* sprang from my continuing passion. I still enjoy talking about old recorders, forgotten studios, and their clunky but beautiful older gear. The book is a first cousin of my previous work, *Too Hot to Handle: An Illustrated Encyclopedia of American Recording Studios of the Twentieth Century.* A soon-to-be-published second edition will feature additional studios, a new cover, new art and photographs, and more information from audio engineers and record-business operatives. Because it is practically a new book, I will brand it *Vintage Recording Studios.* It will be the companion of *Vintage Tape Recorders.* I worked on both books simultaneously over the years, because studios and recorders and gear all converge at some point. When I first wrote and published *Too Hot* in 2001, I had no idea that it would turn into a minor cult book and remain in print eighteen years later. (See Amazon.com.) I published it through my own imprint, HHP Books, because I assumed that no conventional publisher would be interested. Unfortunately, a month after the book was printed, an editor friend called and asked me why I didn't give him a chance to do it. Now, I don't look back. I'm still hearing from assorted gearheads, record collectors, audio engineers, studio owners, music historians, and all manner of people who are interested in recording as well as in America's classic hits. They should like *Vintage Tape Recorders*, too.

The first question people ask me is how long I worked on the books, assuming a year or two at the most. I shake my head in disbelief. I have been saving related printed matter, information, and photographs for twenty-five years, until finally one day I decided to assemble it all as the studio book, and, now, finally, the recorder book. My work on the manuscripts evolved into an even better appreciation for historic recording studios, their hits, vintage gear, house bands, affiliated song-publishing companies, and anything relevant about America's houses of hits and misses. In short, I celebrated the old recorders and equipment that were used from the late 1940s through the early 1990s. My work came in big spurts, and in the process, *Too Hot* became a true labor of lust. How else can I describe it? I salivated over the idea of rediscovering old tapes (some of them my own), creaky studios, older audio engineers, and assorted pieces of our recording past. I visited many studios, some of which had their original equipment stored in back rooms. Imagine my surprise to find an old one-track Ampex recorder stored in a converted rest room! "Hey! What's this?" I shouted from the room. The studio owner shouted back, "History, man!"

Recorders fascinated me long before I received my little AIWI. They first caught my ear when I was a child. On visits to WLWT, the Cincinnati television station from which *The Midwestern Hayride* originated, I became fascinated with tape recorders. I assume that they were two-trackers at that time. My mother used to take me there once a year to visit a friend, who asked one of her audio guys to escort me around the station. I enjoyed watching the big reels spin.

As I went reeling through the years, right into high school, my father helped me start my own "radio" station in my bedroom. He stretched a copper wire from my window to the garage. Voila—a horizontal antenna! My friends helped me broadcast, play tapes, and hope that our programs might reach beyond the garage. The guys had all received similar recorders, so we had three of those things spinning at once. Unbeknownst to us, we were keeping up with the times—three "tracks." Then, disaster struck. My grouchy next-door neighbor picked up our signal on his new color television. That's when my father had to shut down WBOY. But the tape recorders remained, offering endless hours of enjoyment to some kids in Hamilton, Ohio.

My first visits to recording studios began a few weeks after I had graduated from high school in 1966. I stopped in a funky little studio in town and asked the owner-engineer if I could sit in and absorb the lingo and environment. Sure, he said. As I recall, the place had an Ampex two-track machine. The guy was accommodating. He even invited me to sit in the control room during sessions. Anecdotes from engineers and producers became priceless nuggets to me. I began to see my collection of vinyl records from the viewpoint of the people who made them. The ghosts of recording past beckoned me to keep their memories alive. Even then, I had no interest in learning more about electronics or becoming an audio engineer. I just wanted to produce records.

Today, older recorders and their gear still fascinate me. They are a part of what I call the mystique of the studio. You don't feel it when you step into someone's garage or basement studio. I'm just as disappointed when I walk into a larger studio and see only a computer, a console, and a bunch of wires and small black boxes. I always expect to see a big recorder or two. In this era of high-tech recording and computers, however, tape recorders are getting harder to find. The old two-track recorders of the 1950s seem like tools from the Dark Ages. But don't underestimate their effectiveness. They worked—and well. Probably many of the younger readers won't share my enthusiasm, for they didn't live in a time when studios were what I call palaces of sound. I looked on them as magical places that created the music of my times. Back in the 1960s, in the days of flower power, miniskirts, and hippies, I used to wonder: What happens behind closed studio doors? How do the hits originate? What stories do the engineers tell? Surely, I once thought, studios must be other-worldly places that capture the fleeting sounds of indigenous and pleasing music. How else could so many popular sounds emerge on vinyl?

Eventually, I began traveling across the country to visit studios with reputations as hit-making machines. I had high expectations. To my surprise, however, many studios were often nondescript and unassuming. A high-end one in Los Angeles didn't even have a name on it. Other studios were downright funky, particularly the ones in out-of-the-way places. They ranged from ramshackle to rudimentary. But, oh, those tape machines! I didn't care if the owners had to stuff Tampons into the ceiling to stop the rain from leaking inside, as it did in the first Muscle Shoals Sound Studios. I didn't mind if the rooms were hotter than a Mississippi griddle. They were all special studios that created the hits—clear, clean, smooth sounds that have lasted for decades. The proof is in the product. The product often came from outdated tape recorders that still managed to make music sound special.

Because I made records in Ohio, where some rock hits of the 1960s and '70s were born, I'm interested in learning more about the studios and music of Middle America. Most people who are interested in old studios have heard of Cleveland Recording, where Grand Funk Railroad cut its early albums with producer Terry Knight in downtown Cleveland. In those days, the city was a busy regional rock 'n' roll radio capital that had just turned national. Cleveland Recording was at the center of the action. But how many people have heard of Cleveland's Kelmar Studios, at 1054 E. 71st Street? In rock's heyday of 1966, when the Outsiders were cutting "Time Won't Let Me" and other hit singles over at Cleveland Recording, the unheralded Kelmar was operating as a "competitor" of Cleveland Recording—well, sort. Or how about a few other studios in the city then—Way-Out Studios (now there's another great name for a '60s studio), at 1850 E. 55th Street. Then there was Szappanos, at 3046 E. 123rd Street. And how about Boddie, 12202 Union Avenue, and even WBKR Radio, at 1169 Sylvania Road?

Whenever I saw the name of a studio that I had never heard of, I immediately wondered what type of tape machine it had. I still get a laugh from reading the name of a studio with an odd or catchy or emphatically regional name, such as Cavern Sound, founded in 1965 in Independence, Missouri, and Red Flame Recording Studios, founded in 1960 in that state. La Louisianne Studios, founded in 1954 at 711 Stevenson Street in Lafayette, Louisiana, was still in business in the early 1970s. Another favorite was Mo-Do, founded in 1967 (no doubt the brother of MoJo) at 50 Orange Street in Buffalo. Also in New York,

Ultra-Sonic Recording Studios opened in 1963 at 100 N. Franklin Street in Hempstead. There is something special about the name Ultra-Sonic—right out of 1963 and the space program of the era.

As I collected each studio's name and the types of recorders, I realized I was doing it mainly for the sake of history and respect. We're talking about a different world in those days. Remember that these early studios that opened before 1965 operated with fewer than four tracks. Down in New Orleans, engineer-studio owner Cosimo Matassa cut some great recordings on one track. They are tributes to the professionalism of the engineers and the "low-tech" equipment of the era. The way I see it, America sent a man to the moon in 1969, so we had to be doing something right without using much of what gearheads would call high-tech equipment.

Often America's small studios were popular gathering places for musicians, songwriters, audio engineers and wanna-be engineers—the magicians who made the most of only a few tracks. I remember interviewing the songwriter-producer Dan Penn, who owned Beautiful Sounds in Memphis in the early 1970s. Dan said one of his all-time favorite recorders was a three-track machine on which he worked at American Sound Studios. This Memphis studio turned out dozens of national hits, including "The Letter" by the Box Tops, which Penn produced in 1967. He believes the three-track was one of the greatest early tape recorders ever made, and a pleasure to use. Of course, the machine had its detractors, too. When King Records owner Sydney Nathan decided to buy a three-tracker instead of waiting a few months to get a new four-track machine, producer and A&R man Henry Glover became so frustrated that he quit. He had recommended that Nathan go to four tracks. Of course, other issues were percolating between Henry and the Boss, but the three-tracker was a big deal. I have never worked on a three-track machine, but I would love to try one. If Dan Penn liked it, what can I say? I've heard some producers complain about it, but the way I see it, Penn ought to know. In those times, recording technology hadn't developed to the point that good studios could be found in basements on about any block in the country, and, for that matter, in any conceivable place. If you wanted a professional sound—or even close to one—you had to pay good money to rent a studio and hire an engineer to do the sound work in one of the major music centers. Most smaller-town studios had engineers that came with the package. When I booked my first session at Jewel Recording Studios in suburban Cincinnati in 1969, I was amazed at what I believed to be the high cost—from $55 to $75 an hour. Now, $75 an hour was a lot of money to me back then. It still is. But somehow I pulled it together and cut my first record, "Mr. Bus Driver" by Wayne Perry, on a $500 budget. I stepped into the magical room and fulfilled a dream. I was an independent producer. (See Amazon.com or CD Baby for my complication album *Souled Out: Queen City Soul-Rockers of the 1970s.*)

I realize that a recording history is something I had to write. Naturally, at the heart of every studio was the tape recorder. That heart beat steadily throughout America for years.

For those unfamiliar with studio development, here is a brief history that's necessary to put this story into context. The recording studio began with the earliest of recordings. In the late 1800s and early 1900s, acoustic recording "laboratories" were no more than offices where singers sang and musicians played into metal, acoustical recording horns. Technology changed in 1925, when electric recording—with microphones, no less—revolutionized sound and the industry. Soon, recording engineers were experimenting with sound-deadening curtains and walls. They used recording machines that cut grooves into master discs. When Ampex introduced its early tape-recording machines in the late 1940s, the industry further changed. More independent studios—including the King Records studio in Cincinnati and Matassa's J & M Recording in New Orleans—started cutting hits in country music and rhythm and blues. The larger cities, of course, had their established studios in which commercials and recordings were made. As advancements were made in tape machines, more studios spread across the country and more tracks—two, three, four, eight, sixteen, twenty-four—were added.

The American recording studio peaked in prestige and importance in the late-1970s and early 1980s. Some years later, more affordable, digital equipment overtook the business. Today, it is difficult to tell the difference between a home studio and a professional one—or, for that matter, from one recording to another. So many sounds are homogeneous. So many are electronic. Many of the older studios have gone out of business, and their studio players have gone home to wash their cars and wait for session calls that come all too infrequently. Their clients no longer need them. The industry has changed drastically. In this book, I concentrate primarily on preserving the *visual*—photographs, advertisements, spec sheets, and handbills—to help commemorate our nation's vintage recorders, gear, gizmos, and studios. Like the first book, I offer studios from the golden days of tape recording—the 1950s through the 1970s. Studios in the megacities are fine, but they have been chronicled before. I prefer to search for lesser-known studios and for the smaller ones that contributed—no matter how little—in communities that weren't necessarily known for recording. (I love the name of this one: Laboratory of Jax, a studio that operated in the mid-1960s at 1104 South Edgewood Avenue in Jacksonville, Florida.) Naturally, this book is filled with tape recorder information. I've tried to show the old ads in larger size, so you can read what engineers had to know sixty-some years ago.

We salute them all—one, two, three, four, eight, sixteen, twenty-four tracks. Anything analog will do for me. I still record on a twenty-four track Otari, but those old machines are getting harder to find, at least those in working order. So let us pause for a moment to also salute magnetic tape, mono mixes, *real* echo chambers, and the rigged-up, slap-back of Sam Phillips and Sun Records. We salute our vintage recording heritage. Long may it live!

Randy McNutt
April 30, 2019

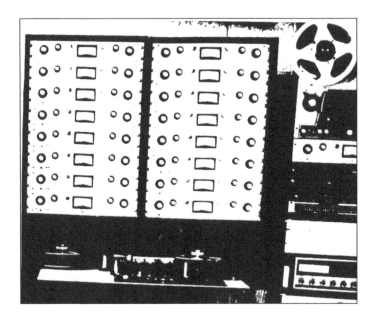

From the Brians Studio in Tyler, Texas:
Sixteen tracks and cooking, c. 1968.

Allied catalog items, 1956.

In 1952, RCA was going after its share of the new tape and related sound market.

By the summer of '49, the long-used transcription disc was a primary target of magnetic recording tape. Even new microgroove transcription discs were not immune. Surprisingly, the transcription disc would stick around in a lesser capacity for years. It was still a convenient method of presenting radio programs—at least until tape finally became the accepted medium for such shows.

More grooves in the bands, 1950s.

II.

Vintage Audio Advertising
1948-1970

*The vital key to fidelity in your tape recordings
is the microphone. The quality of the entire performance
hinges on the ability of the microphone to translate with
supreme accuracy the living, breathing reality of the words
and music you put into it.*

Electro-Voice advertisement
April 1956

Model 510-B   MAGNEMASTER *

1949

TWIN-TRAX * RECORDER
The Popular-Priced Rack Mount
MAGNETIC TAPE RECORDER
With Broadcast Fidelity

A brand new version of the famous *Twin-Trax Recorder*, dynamically balanced for vertical operation with negligible flutter and wow, and mounted in a handsome chrome trimmed rack cabinet. Specifications that are fully professional, yet sold to you *direct from the factory* at easy-on-the-budget prices. And economical to operate, because *Twin-Trax Recorders* use two sound tracks on standard half-hour reels of magnetic tape. Result is twice the playing time; one-half the tape cost.

The combination of the advanced-design mechanical chassis and a wide range 10-tube recording-playback amplifier will provide musical recording and reproduction completely satisfactory for rigid broadcast requirements. A 6 x 9 GE Monitor Speaker completes the installation. A 6E5 Volume Indicator is included on the control panel, and a built-in socket is provided for optionally available recording and output level VU meters.

You can use this equipment to replace or augment expensive transcription equipment. Traditional Amplifier Corp. of America high quality workmanship, unusual performance, and specifications that appeal to the engineer.

List Price	$580.00
Professional Net Price	$435.00

GENERAL SPECIFICATIONS:

TUBES SUPPLIED:	(1) 12SJ7; (1) 12SC7; (1) 6SL7GT; (2) 6SN7GT; (3) 6V6GT; (1) 6E5; (1) 5Y3GT
FREQUENCY RANGE:	50 to 9,000 cycles ± 2 db.
PLAYING TIME:	1 hour.
TAPE SPEED:	7½ inches per second.
DYNAMIC RANGE:	50 db.
INPUT CHANNELS:	Microphone and Radio-phono.
INPUT IMPEDANCE:	Microphone 1 Meg. Radio-Phono ½ Meg.
HI-FREQUENCY CONTROL RANGE:	From + 13 db. to —10 at 9,000 cycles.
LOW-FREQUENCY CONTROL RANGE:	From + 9½ db. to —6½ db. at 50 cycles.
MINIMUM SIGNAL:	(High Gain Input) 0.001 Volts.
MINIMUM SIGNAL:	(Medium Gain Input) 0.01 Volts.
EXTERNAL CONNECTIONS FOR:	Headphones; External Speaker; Booster Amplifier; 500/600 ohm line.
ERASE AND BIAS FREQUENCY:	50 kc.
NUMBER OF TAPE PLAYBACKS:	More than 5,000.
SPEED VARIATIONS (INSTANTANEOUS):	±0.1%.
AMPLITUDE VARIATIONS (1,000 cycles):	0.75 db.
TOTAL DISTORTION:	Less than 3%.
NUMBER OF RE-RECORDINGS:	More than 5,000.
RIBBON SPLICING:	With Scotch Tape.
TAPE REVERSAL:	Automatic
ERASURE:	Automatic
FORWARD & REVERSE SHUTTLE SPEED:	30 inches per second.
LINE VOLTAGE:	105/120 Volts AC 60 cycles.
POWER CONSUMPTION:	135 Watts.
DIMENSIONS:	28" H; 21⅜" W; 15" D.
NET WEIGHT:	85 lbs.
MODEL No.:	510B.
LIST PRICE:	$580.00.
PROFESSIONAL NET PRICE:	$435.00.

SPECIAL TWIN-TRAX FEATURES

1. One Hour of Continuous Recording on Standard ½ hour reels.
2. Individual Bass and Treble Tone Controls.
3. Simplified Tape Threading. No Intertwining.
4. Heavy-duty non-overheating motor.
5. No rewinding necessary. Continuous forward and reverse travel.
6. Automatic tape reversal at end of reel.
7. Low hum level (DC on input heaters).
8. Socket for VU meter.
9. All major components easily accessible.
10. Instantaneous reverse control—without unthreading tape.
11. Instantaneous stop—no syllable or note slurring
12. High speed forward and reverse shuttle without unthreading.
13. No tape spillage possible during high speed shuttle.
14. Plays single track recordings made on other tape recorders.
15. Rubber rimmed drive cannot develop flats.
16. Complete elimination of tape slippage.
17. 3.2 and 500/600 ohm balanced line outputs.
18. Jack provided for earphone monitoring.
19. Twin electronic erase heads for separate channel erasure.
20. Precision tape speed drive assures negligible flutter and wow.
21. No belts to loosen or pulleys to slip.
22. Quiet mechanical operation.

Four-hour continuous play. Special unit for applications requiring longer than one hour of continuous operation. Same professional specifications and desirable features as Model 510B, but also equipped with auxiliary drive mechanism which will accommodate larger reels to provide up to four hours of continuous recording and playback. Will also play standard one hour reels. Rack cabinet size 42⅞" H; 22" W; 15¼" D.

Model 520B

Model 520B List Price	$795.00
Professional Net Price	$595.00

Note: All standard accessories available for these rack mount recorders.

Order direct from

MAGNEPHONE DIVISION

AMPLIFIER CORP. of AMERICA
396 Broadway • New York 13, N. Y.

Trade Mark

CIRCULAR No. 5034   PRINTED IN U.S.A.   Copyright 1949 AMPLIFIER CORP. OF AMERICA

Amplifier Corporation of America was one of the early makers of tape records. This one is from 1949.

Location Recorders, an early mobile recording company, c. 1970.

Now...record the *whole* performance...
without a break!

YOU'LL GET EVERY NOTE of your favorite concert broadcast, sports event or dramatic program when you put it on new "Scotch" Brand Extra Play Magnetic Tape 190. Half as thick as conventional tapes but made with strength to spare, new Extra Play tape offers *50% more recording time* on a standard size reel. Thus, annoying interruptions for reel change are reduced to a minimum.

"Scotch" Brand's exclusive new oxide dispersion process gives you more brilliant sound, too. By packing fine-grain oxide particles into a neat, thin pattern, "Scotch" Brand has been able to produce a super-sensitive, high-potency magnetic recording surface on Extra Play Magnetic Tape. Hear the difference yourself. Try new "Scotch" Brand Extra Play Magnetic Tape 190 on your machine *today*.

EXTRA-THIN. 50% thinner, more potent oxide coating, 30% thinner backing permit more 190 Tape to be wound on standard-size reel. Result: one roll of new tape does job of 1½ reels of ordinary tape.

ELECTRON PHOTO microscope shows the difference! At left, artist's conception of view of old-style oxide coating. At right, "SCOTCH" Brand's new dispersion process lays oxide in neat, fine-grain pattern.

SCOTCH BRAND *Extra Play* Magnetic Tape 190

The term "SCOTCH" and the plaid design are registered trademarks for Magnetic Tape made in U.S.A. by MINNESOTA MINING AND MFG. CO., St. Paul 6, Minn. Export Sales Office: 99 Park Avenue, New York 16, N.Y.

Scotch, anyone? The venerable Scotch tape in its early days, the 1950s.

As magnetic tape recorders took hold in the early 1950s,
Fairchild's transcriptions continued for a time.
Above, the magnetic tape eraser entered the market.

African Torture Test
proves LR audiotape immune to extreme heat and humidity

By the mid-1950s, Mylar polyester recording tape had hit the market.

8 KEYS TO PERFECT SOUND

▶ There's an Audiotape for every recording job — eight types, each with the famous quality and uniformity that give top performance on any recorder

it speaks for itself

AUDIO DEVICES, INC., 444 Madison Ave., N. Y. 22, N. Y.

In Hollywood: 840 N. Fairfax Ave. • In Chicago: 5428 Milwaukee Ave.
Export Dept.: 13 East 40th St., N. Y., 16 • Cables "ARLAB"
Rectifier Division: 620 E. Dyer Rd., Santa Ana, Calif.

PLASTIC-BASE AUDIOTAPE on 1½-mil cellulose acetate meets the most exacting requirements of the professional, educational and home recordist at minimum cost. Known the world over for matchless performance and consistent uniform quality. Series 51, in the red box.

AUDIOTAPE ON 1½-MIL MYLAR * — a premium-quality professional tape with maximum mechanical strength and immunity to heat and humidity. Will not dry out or embrittle with age. Series 71, in the green box.

"LR" AUDIOTAPE ON 1-MIL "MYLAR" — 50% more recording time per reel. Strong, super-durable polyester film base assures trouble-free operation even under extreme heat and humidity. Series 61, in the black-and-red box.

PLASTIC-BASE "LR" AUDIOTAPE provides 50% more recording time on low-cost 1-mil cellulose acetate base, affording maximum economy where high strength is not required. Series 41, in the blue box.

SUPER-THIN AUDIOTAPE on ½-mil "Mylar" gives twice as much recording time per reel as standard plastic-base tape. For long-play applications where tape tension is not excessive. Series 31, in the yellow box.

SUPER-THIN AUDIOTAPE ON TEMPERED "MYLAR" gives twice as much recording time per reel as conventional tape and is *twice as strong* as other double-length tapes. Will not stretch or break on any tape recorder — will not dry out or embrittle with age. Series 31 T, in the black-red-and-yellow box.

MASTER LOW PRINT-THROUGH AUDIOTAPE on plastic base — reduces print-through (magnetic echo) by 8 db. The finest, professional-quality recording tape. Base material, 1½-mil acetate. Maximum fidelity, uniformity, frequency response and freedom from noise and distortion . Series 51M, in the red-and-gold box.

MASTER LOW PRINT-THROUGH AUDIOTAPE on 1½-mil "Mylar" — print-through (magnetic echo) is reduced by 8 db. A super durable tape that meets the highest standards of performance. Withstands extreme temperatures and is virtually immune to humidity. Has maximum life under any conditions . Series 71M, in the green-and-gold box. *DuPont Trade Mark*

By the middle of the 1950s, Mylar was all over the place. "It speaks for itself," the slogan claimed.

In the 1950s, Electro-Voice is a leading microphone for tape recording and on-stage performances.

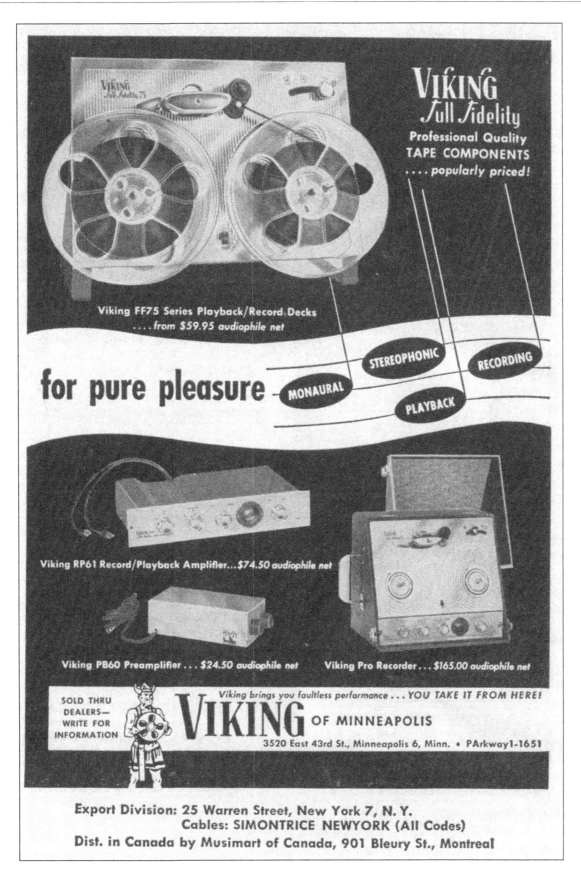

A Viking recorder, mid-1950s.

here's why you get
EXTRA LENGTH
plus
EXTRA STRENGTH

with **LR audiotape** on **Mylar** polyester film

NOW YOU can get the *extra length* that many tape recording applications require, without any sacrifice in strength or durability. For the new Type LR Audiotape, made on 1-mil "Mylar," actually has greater impact, tensile and tear strength than even the conventional plastic-base tape of 50% greater thickness.

And because "Mylar" withstands extreme temperatures and is virtually immune to humidity, LR Audiotape stands up longer under the most severe conditions of use and storage.

This Longer Recording Audiotape is now available in 900, 1800 and 3600-ft. reels. Audio also offers a complete standard line of Audiotape on "Mylar," in 1, 1½ and 2-mil base thickness. Test it—compare it with any other tape on the market. In *performance* and *durability*, it speaks for itself!

Table I	TESTS AT 75°F, 50% RELATIVE HUMIDITY	
	Yield Strength	Breaking Strength
1 mil Acetate	3.7 lb.	3.9 lb.
0.9 mil "Mylar"	4.2 lb.	7.6 lb.
1.45 mil Acetate	5.0 lb.	5.5 lb.

Table II	TESTS AT 75°F, 90% RELATIVE HUMIDITY	
	Yield Strength	Breaking Strength
1 mil Acetate	1.8 lb.	2.5 lb.
0.9 mil "Mylar"	4.1 lb.	7.6 lb.
1.45 mil Acetate	3.0 lb.	4.1 lb.

The above test data, taken under conditions of both winter and summer humidity, show the marked superiority of 1-mil "Mylar," not only over the thin cellulose acetate base, but over the standard 1.45-mil acetate as well.

*Dupont Trade Mark

HOME RECORDISTS — CHURCH RECORDISTS:

Enter Audio Devices' *BIG PRIZE CONTESTS* for the best articles on "How I Use My Tape Recorder."

WIN a V-M "tape-o-matic" recorder, plus $100 cash, plus 20 7-inch reels of Audiotape. Ten other valuable awards, too!

Contest closes April 1, 1955. See your Audiotape dealer, or write to Audio Devices today for complete details. There's nothing to buy!

AUDIO DEVICES, Inc.

444 Madison Avenue, New York 22, N. Y.
Offices in Hollywood • Chicago
Export Dept., 13 E. 40th St., N. Y. 16, N. Y., Cables "ARLAB"

By the mid-1950s, new tape companies are popping up. Here is L R magnetic audio tape.

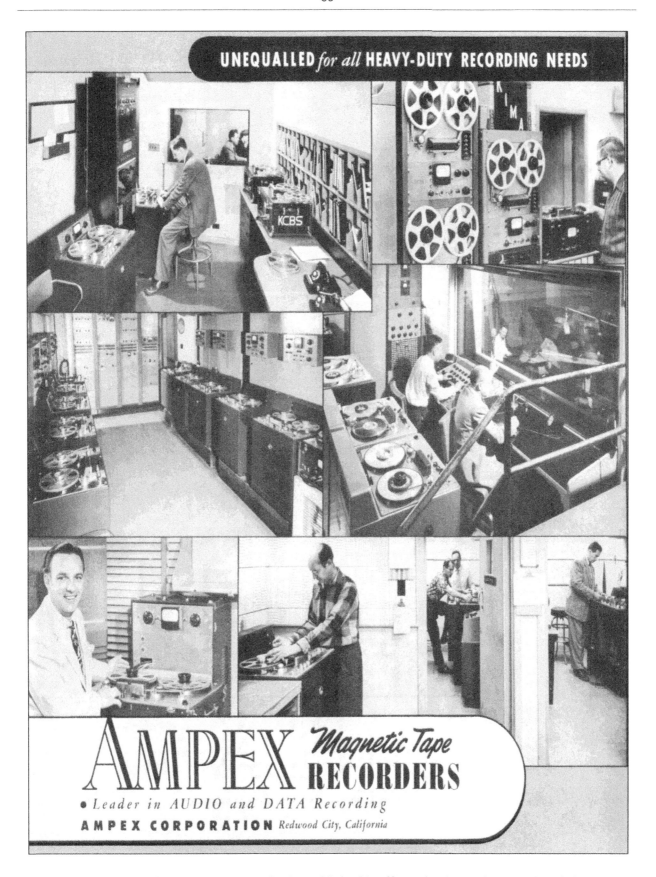

By the mid- to late-1950s, Ampex had established itself as a leader in the recording field.

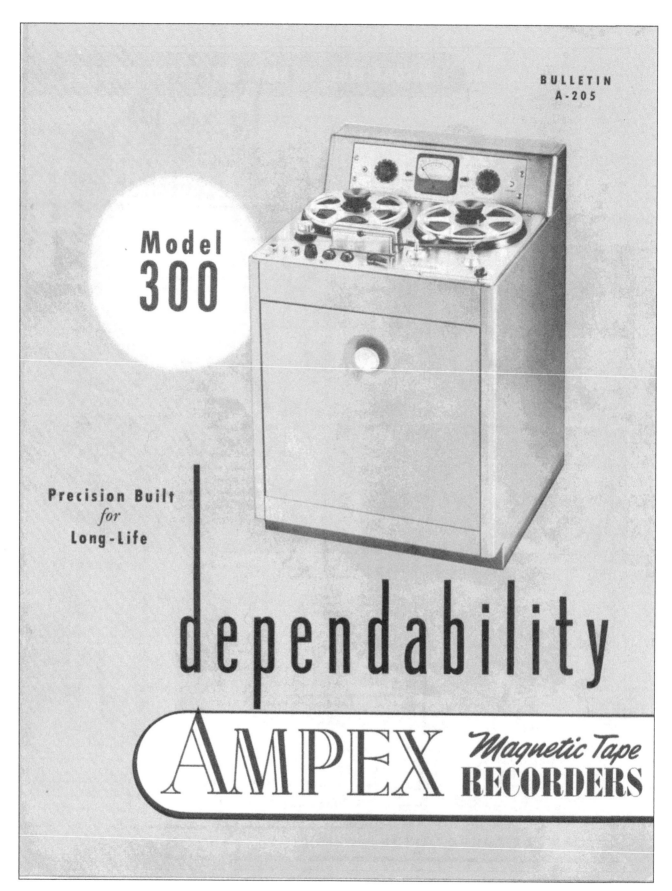

Model
300

Precision Built
for
Long-Life

dependability

AMPEX *Magnetic Tape* RECORDERS

In the early 1950s, the Ampex 300 became a workhorse in recording and television studios. Many hit records were cut on the 300. It remained a staple of the studio business for years.

When C. Robert Fine spoke, people listened. He was a studio entrepreneur with clout in the '50s. C. Robert Fine was a leader in New York's recording studio business. His Fine Recording Studio was a major destination for clients in and out of the city.

HERE IS THE TAPE RECORDER
THAT "COULDN'T BE MADE"...

What a serious high-fidelity enthusiast wants in a tape recorder has never been a mystery. He wants a recorder which, at 7½ ips will equal or exceed professional performance at 15 ips and at a price comparable to the price of the usual garden variety of "home recorder" In other words, he wants flat response over the entire audio range, undetectable noise, hum, wow and flutter and professional NARTB equalization at 7½ ips (to give up to 90 minutes of playing time on a 7" reel at a cost lower than one good LP record) and all for less than $300.

Now, DeJUR, a great name in high-quality precision cameras, answers the demands of the HiFi enthusiast in every particular. For the first time in America, he can have a tape recorder meeting his most exacting performance requirements for a fraction of the price he would normally expect to pay.

Compare it in an A-B test with the most expensive professional recorder your high-fidelity outlet carries. We're that sure you won't be able to tell the difference!

Now, let's get down to specifications. They have been checked by an independent engineering firm and confirmed by the testing laboratories of America's largest high-fidelity distributors.

FREQUENCY RESPONSE

At 7½ ips, the frequency response is 40 cps to 16,000 cps ± 2 db (the closest comparable machine is 1,000 cps *less* and $100 more!) Even at 3¾ ips, the DeJUR Dual Professional is flat from 50 cps to 10,000 cps ± 2 db.

SIGNAL-TO-NOISE RATIO

Noise is down 55 db (that equals or exceeds the figure for recorders priced at $600 and up!)

FLUTTER AND WOW

The DeJUR Dual Professional uses a heavy-duty genuine hysteresis dual-speed, synchronous motor, the same type of motor used in $1,000 studio recorders (even the better "home recorders" use only 4-pole motors!) A hysteresis motor is independent of line voltage fluctuations, thus eliminating a major source of wow and flutter Both

are less than 0.1% at 7½ ips, 0.2% at 3¾ ips (the competitive recorder closest in performance has 0.25% at 7½ ips and costs $100 more!)

EQUALIZATION

Professional NARTB equalization is used throughout the DeJUR Dual Professional. This means that, not only can you make and play back tapes of perfect fidelity, but you can also play commercial pre-recorded tapes the way they were *meant* to be played.

INSTANT TRACK SWITCHING

Four separate heads are employed in the Dual Professional an erase head and a record-playback head for each track. When you reach the end of a reel on the first track, you simply press a button and the tape reverses its motion recording or playing back the second track! Anyone who has fussed and fumed as he tried to change reels in the middle of a symphony will greet this feature with cheers!

ELECTROMAGNETIC DYNAMIC BRAKING

In the DeJUR Dual Professional, there are no mechanical clutches, belts and pulleys to get out of order. The dual speed hysteresis motor is reversible and electromagnetic dynamic braking is employed for instantaneous stops and starts without tape strain or stress.

ILLUMINATED TAPE COUNTER

An illuminated, clock-like dial indicates elapsed footage so accurately that the tape can be indexed to a single note!

AUTOMATIC STOP

Inexpensive DeJUR aluminum foil leaders are available which automatically stop tape motion in either direction! There's no need to re-thread no flopping tape ends.

PUSH-BUTTON KEYBOARD

A piano key switchboard controls all recording and playback functions through relays. Even your wife can operate the DeJUR Dual Professional without an instruction manual!

OTHER EXCEPTIONAL FEATURES

Instantaneous stopping in record or

playback, less than ¼" in fast wind; 2 high impedance and 1 low impedance inputs controlled by selector switch, rewind time of 90 seconds for 1200-foot reel in either direction, foam rubber pressure rollers, relay operated and triple-fused for protection against improper operation, 105-220 volt, 60 cycle AC operation.

And the price? That's the biggest surprise of all! The DeJUR Dual Professional Tapedeck is only $299.50 audiophile net!

Also available in a handsome, scuff-proof carrying case complete with built-in 6-watt power amplifier, 2 electrostatic speakers, 3 PM speakers and wide-range cardioid dynamic microphone for only $379.50 audiophile net!

AVAILABLE ACCESSORIES

Remote control foot switch $19.50.
Wide-range cardioid microphone $29.50.

WRITE FOR COMPLETE SPECIFICATIONS

DeJUR-AMSCO CORPORATION
Dept. TR-1, Long Island City 1, N. Y

NOTHING COMPARES WITH A

DeJUR (DeJUR USA)

Dual Professional

TAPE RECORDER

The DeJur company was yet another name in 1950s tape recording. The firm made recorders for home use as well as professional use, but its main market was the more sophisticated amateur.

Soundcraft was another big name in manufacturing recording tape, starting in the 1950s.

Though not as popular as Scotch, Livingston tape prospered. This ad is from the late 1950s. The company catered more to high-end home use.

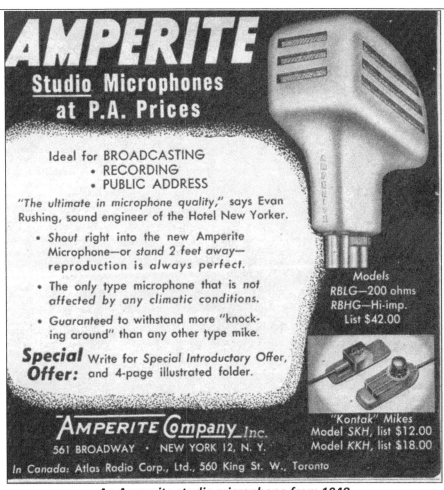

An Amperite studio microphone from 1948.

Some 1950s tape enthusiasts—or recordists.

It was a tube world back then, and in 1950 Sylvania was one of its kings.
If you recorded, you had to deal with tubes.

Producer-engineer Steve Jerome at the console at World United Studio, N.Y., c. 1965. Left, owner Hash Brown, a New York musician, with Reparata and the Delrons. Producer Bill Jerome looks on during a session for World Artists Records of Pittsburgh.

Margaret Whiting records in the Capitol Studios, New York, c. 1951. Note the talk-back mic and console.

One can imagine a 1955 roadhouse owner grabbing an E-V mic from a singer and shouting, "Stop throwing the beer bottles!"

Berlant, a recording pioneer, offers a machine aimed at broadcasters,
while Crown does the same thing. Both from the mid-1950s.

Elgin Watch Company got into the manufacturing of microphones for tape recorders in the early 1950s.

As the 1950s reached the halfway point, Ampex was promoting its new 600 model, which was described as a semi-professional recorder. It was used by amateurs and pros alike.

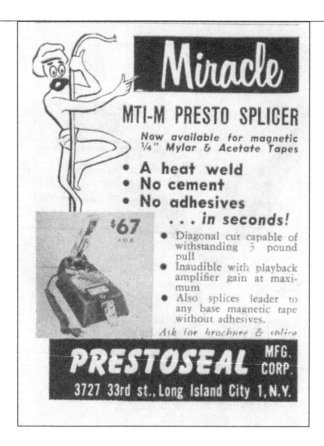

The tape splicer was becoming important for recordists in the early 1950s. The one below is from 1955.

Les Paul and Mary Ford went electric, with guitars and an experimental multi-track tape recorder.

By the mid- to late-1960s, Scully was promoting its two-track workhorse.

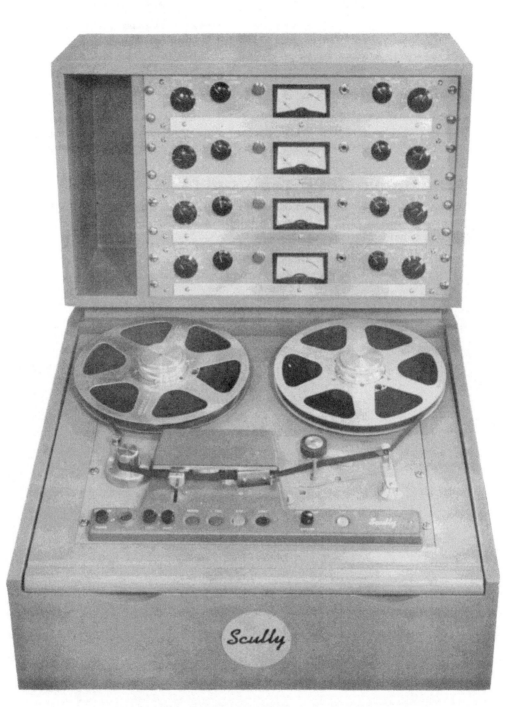

SCULLY   MODEL   280   TAPE   RECORDER
Four channel ½ inch professional tape recorder
Price....$3,950 f.o.b. Bridgeport, Connecticut
Technical specifications on request

SCULLY RECORDING INSTRUMENTS CORPORATION
480 Bunnell Street, Bridgeport, Conn.

A four-track Scully spec sheet, mid-1960s, for dealers and recording studios. Details on the next page.

Interchangeable Plug-in Head Assemblies

Exclusive Scully 280 feature permits rapid interchange from four track to three track head assembly. Scully precision machining allows this head assembly change without azimuth adjustment. Your half inch machine now does the work of two . . . and does it better!

Built-in Selective Sync

Now . . . at no additional cost . . . built-in selective synchronization on all three and four track half-inch units . . . permits switching of any record track to playback cueing while recording on other channels. Another reason why Scully is the best buy in professional recorders.

Adjustable Width Tape Guides

Another Scully exclusive . . . adjustable width tape guides permits rapid interchange from half-inch to quarter-inch tape widths, utilizing the plug-in feature of Scully head assemblies. Available at slight additional cost.

- Front panel electronic calibration and alignment

- Equalization change on speed selector switch

- Individual reel size switches

- Front panel termination switch

- Scully designed scrape filter

- 100% solid state

Prices

Model 282-4 four channel half-inch recorder/reproducer	$3945
Plug-in three channel head assembly	586
Adjustable width tape guides, per pair	35
Walnut grained formica console mount	280
Four track portable carrying case	215

SCULLY RECORDING INSTRUMENTS CORPORATION
480 Bunnell Street, Bridgeport, Conn., Tel. (203) 335-5146

EXCLUSIVE EXPORT AGENTS:
ROCKE INTERNATIONAL CORP., 13 EAST 40th ST., NEW YORK, N.Y. CABLES: ARLAB

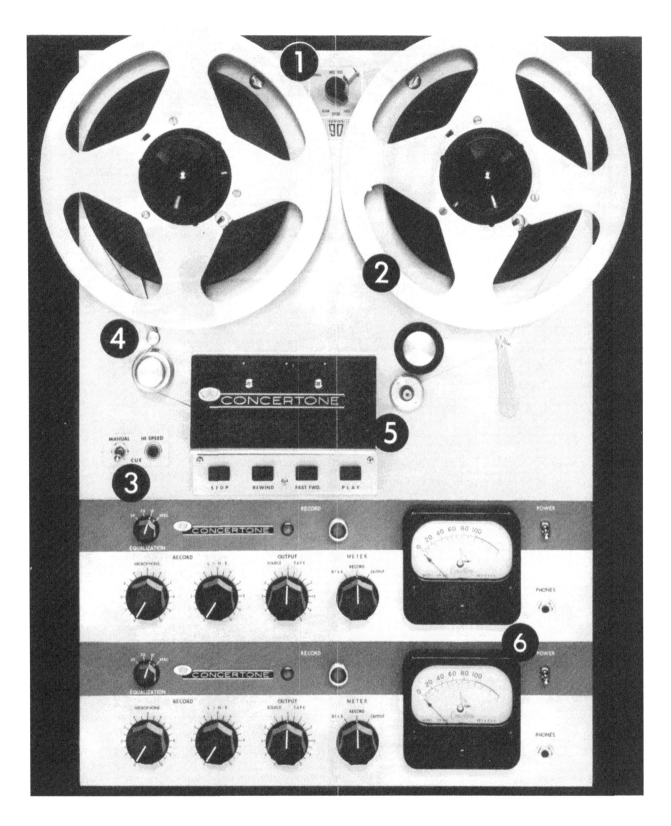

A strikingly handsome two-track Concertone, late-1950s.

Professional features found in the Series 90, bring recording perfection and versatility previously unheard of, except in the costliest tape recorders.

- ■ Record Indicator Lights
- ■ A B Monitoring
- ■ Relay-Solenoid Operation
- ■ Optional Remote Control
- ■ Two- or four-track stereo
- ■ Automatic Cut-Off
- ■ Automatic Tape Lifters
- ■ Front Panel Equalization Control
- ■ Cannon Connectors
- ■ Built-in 600 Ohm Output

SPECIFICATIONS

TAPE SPEEDS
7.5 — 15 ips or 3.75 — 7.5 ips. A third speed may be obtained by pulley change.

TIMING ACCURACY
99.9% or better over 1 hour run.

FREQUENCY RESPONSE (OVERALL RESPONSE FOR RECORD AND PLAYBACK)
40—15000 cps ± 2 db at 15 ips
40—12000 cps ± 2 db at 7.5 ips
50—7500 cps ± 2 db at 3.75 ips

SIGNAL TO NOISE RATIO
Full Track: 55 db at 7.5 and 15 ips
50 db at 3.75 ips
Stereo: 50 db at 7.5 and 15 ips (2 & 4 Track)
45 db at 3.75 ips
The peak record level is defined as that level at which the overall (input to output) total RMS harmonic distortion is 2% when measured on a 400 cycle tone. Noise is measured when erasing a signal of peak recording level and in absence of new signal. Thus, bias and erase noise are included as well as playback amplifier noise. All components between 40 and 15,000 cycles are measured.

TOTAL HARMONIC DISTORTION
1% at operating level. 3% 6 db above operating level

CROSSTALK RATIO
50 db

FLUTTER AND WOW
Less than .1% rms at 15 ips
Less than .12% rms at 7.5 ips
Less than .2% rms at 3.75 ips
NOTE: Flutter and wow measurements include all components between 0 and 300 cps using an RMS value of constant amplitude sine wave flutter.

PLAYING TIME WITH NAB 10½" REELS 2400 FT. OF TAPE

Speed	Half Track	Full Track
15 ips	64 min.	32 min.
7½ ips	2 hrs. 8 min.	64 min.
3¾ ips	4 hrs. 16 min.	2 hrs. 8 min.

REWIND & FAST FORWARD
Approximately 90 seconds for 2400 ft. NAB reel; 30 seconds for 1200 ft. EIA reel. Rewind times for thin base tapes proportionately longer.

START AND STOP TIME
.5 second

CONTROLS
Tape motion controlled by four push buttons; Start, Stop, Fast forward and Rewind. Separate record button energizes record circuits, which drop out when machine is stopped. Individual record button control for each channel in 2 channel stereo machines. All amplifiers are provided with switched equalization for 3 speeds — 3¾, 7½, 15 ips plus a fourth position for any special plug-in equalization modules to any customers' specifications. Motor speed is controlled by a separate switch.

INPUT IMPEDANCE
LINE: High impedance balanced or unbalanced; 600 or 10,000 ohm balanced or unbalanced with plug-in transformers.
MICROPHONE: High impedance unbalanced; 50, 250, or 600 ohm balanced or unbalanced with terminating switch to allow connection to high impedance input.

OUTPUT LEVEL
+ 4 dbm at zero VU; reserve gain to + 8 dbm.

MONITORING
Separate record and playback amplifiers allow tape to be monitored while recording. A high impedance phone jack is provided to monitor either the record input signal before or during recording, or the output signal from the playback. An A—B volume control is incorporated in order that direct comparison can be made between the original program and the recorded program. The meter switch transfers a 4—inch VU meter to indicate output level, and bias current.

POWER REQUIREMENTS
MONOPHONIC RECORDERS:
Approximately 260W, 115v, 60 cps.
STEREO RECORDERS:
Approximately 320W, 115v, 60 cps.

RACK SPACE
Standard 19" wide panel with commercial notching.
TAPE TRANSPORT: 15¾" x 8". Weight, 48 lbs.
AMPLIFIER: 19" x 5¼" x 8¼". Weight, 12 lbs. (Two amplifiers required for 2 channel stereo.)

REMOTE CONTROL
Control is available for remote operation of all models. In stereo systems remote button operates both amplifiers.

AMERICAN CONCERTONE, INC.

A DIVISION OF ASTRO-SCIENCE CORPORATION
9449 WEST JEFFERSON BOULEVARD • CULVER CITY, CALIFORNIA
Telephone: UPton 0-7245

Page two of the Concertone spec sheet shows automatic tape lifters and panel equalization.

Features.....

1 LONG-LIFE MAGNETIC HEADS
(Uniform characteristics during their long life)

2 WIDE RANGE RECORDING
(30 to 15,000 cps at 15 & 7½ inches per second)

3 RELIABLE FAST START
(Full speed in less than 1/10 of a second)

4 SOLENOID PUSH BUTTON OPERATION
(Adaptable for remote control)

5 QUICK ACTING MECHANICAL BRAKES
(On turntable motors)

6 EFFORTLESS TAPE THREADING
("Drop-in" and self-aligning)

7 DEPENDABLE PRECISION TIMING
(Varies less than 3.6 seconds in 30 minutes including tape stretch from humidity and temperature change)

8 EASY EDITING
(Fast operating selector switch)

9 NEGLIGIBLE MAINTENANCE
(Rugged precision drive)

STAYS IN ADJUSTMENT
....*eliminates costly servicing*

HEAVY-DUTY RECORDING
is *EASY* for Model 300!

Ampex Model 300 Recorder completely dominates the heavy-duty recording field. In radio network broadcasting, studio quality recording, show transcription, disc record manufacture and master tape recording of numerous types, Ampex Model 300 has been adopted in preference to other methods and equipment. The reason, complete dependability. This reflects in a very real dollar saving. These savings come from greatly reduced maintenance, elimination of mechanical breakdowns, and negligible out-of-service periods. Many users have more than paid for their Ampex Model 300 out of these sizable savings.

Ampex Model 300 can deliver on these promises because it is a masterpiece in precision manufacture. It has extra capacities in power, ruggedness and wide range recording abilities, making it ideal for grueling continuous service. Superb mechanical stability, together with the finest magnetic heads ever built, faithfully capture wide range tonal qualities of voice and instrument. The precision speeds of the tape transport system successfully avoid objectionable flutter and produces split-second program timing. Studio engineers are able to devote full attention to programming because Ampex Model 300 responds instantly and reliably to its principal modes of operation, either by top plate push-button control or by remote control.

View inside Model 300 . . . note extra rugged construction. Large, quiet ventilating fan removes objectionable heat. Arrangement makes all elements accessible for inspection. Entire cabinet is sound proofed.

Unerrin
CONTINU
Performa

Captures **EVERY** Mood, Le

The front of this Ampex 300 spec sheet, mid-1950s, is featured on two pages.

Realistic Reproduction *Year-after-Year*

The ability of Model 300 to maintain its initial accuracy of motion is largely due to its carefully designed capstan drive. By precision manufacture and rigid unit assembly construction both flutter and mechanical vibration are eliminated. Under continuous duty Model 300's reserve capacity pays off in unequalled recording performance and negligible maintenance and servicing requirements.

**PRECISION DRIVE MOTORS
SPECIALLY BUILT FOR MODEL 300**

FINEST TAPE TRANSPORT MECHANISM *Ever Built for Audio Recording!*

SPECIFICATIONS

All performance characteristics of the Model 300 Magnetic Tape Recorder equal or exceed the standards of the NAB (National Association of Broadcasters). All Ampex audio recorders produce a tape frequency characteristic which has been accepted as standard by NAB.

TAPE SPEED

15 inches per second and 7.5 inches per second, with speed change effected by a single control. The same control also provides the necessary equalization change to compensate for the change in speed.

FREQUENCY RESPONSE

15 inches ±2 db. 30-15,000 cycles. 7½ inches ±4 db. 40-15,000 cycles. ±2 db. 40-10,000 cycles.

SIGNAL-TO-NOISE RATIO

Over 70 db. unweighted noise to maximum recording level. Over 60 db, as defined by NAB standards. By NAB definition, the signal-to-noise ratio is the ratio of peak recording level to the total unweighted playback noise when erasing a signal of peak recording level and in the absence of a new signal. Thus bias and erase noise are included, as well as playback amplifier noise. All frequencies between 50 and 15,000 cycles are measured. The peak recording level is defined as that level at which the overall (input to output) total rms harmonic distortion does not exceed 3% when measured on a 400 cycle tone.

STARTING TIME

Instantaneous. (When starting in the Normal Play mode of operation, the tape is up to full speed in less than 1/10 second.)

STOPPING TIME

When playing at 15 inches per second, tape moves less than 2 inches after depressing Stop button.

FLUTTER AND WOW

At 15 inches per second, well under 0.1% rms, measuring all flutter components from 0 to 300 cycles, using a tone of 3,000 cycles. At 7.5 inches, under 0.2%.

PLAYBACK TIMING ACCURACY

0.2% or ±3.6 seconds for a 30 minute recording.

PLAYING TIME

33 minutes at 15 inch speed on standard NAB reel, 66 minutes at 7.5 inch speed. The Model 300 will also accommodate the standard RMA reel in various thicknesses.

REWIND TIME

One minute for the full NAB reel (2400 feet).

CONTROLS

Start, Stop and Record are push-button, relay operated and may be remote controlled. Normal Play, Fast Forward, and Rewind on a selector switch, with rapid shuttling back and forth made possible by instantly changing from one mode of operation to the other without stopping in between.

COMPLETE PLUG-IN HEAD HOUSING

Double mumetal shield cans on playback head, equivalent shielding on record head, matching self-aligned covers on hinged gate. Drop-in threading.

SIMULTANEOUS MONITORING

Independent record and playback systems allow the tape to be monitored while recording.

RECORD AMPLIFIER

10,000 ohms bridging input, normally set up for +4 VU in balanced or unbalanced.

PLAYBACK AMPLIFIER

Adjusted for +4 VU output, 600 ohms or 150 ohms balanced or unbalanced. Will deliver +20 dbm without exceeding 1% total harmonic distortion at any frequency from 30-15,000 cycles.

DIMENSIONS

Mechanical unit on 24½" panel and Electronic unit on 12¼" panel. For standard rack, console or two case portable mounting.

SHIPPING WEIGHTS AND MOUNTING

Console 270 pounds, 2 Case Portable 175 pounds, Rack 140 pounds.

POWER INPUT REQUIRED

3 amperes, 115 volts, 60 cycles. (Also available for 50 cycles.)

METER CONTROL PANEL

Available at extra cost with features outlined as follows: Mounted on 5¼" panel for rack, console, or portable case mounting. Bridge Input step control will adjust record level for any input greater than —20 VU, 10,000 ohm bridging, any balanced or unbalanced line. Output Step control will adjust level up to +8 VU with normal of tape level — 600 ohm or 150 ohm balanced or unbalanced line. VU meter will meter playback output while recording or playing back. Calibrated for +4 VU output. Output key (line or cue). Phone Jack with input-output key (A-B Key).

MODEL NUMBER		CATALOG NUMBER (115-120 Volt AC)	
		60 cycle	50 cycle
300-C . . . . Console		560-C	3389
300-R . . . . . Rack Mounted		560-R	3390
300-S . . Two Case Portable		560-S	3391

NOTE: *The above Catalog Numbers do not include Control Panel. When ordering Bridging Meter Control Panel specify Catalog Number 515-2.*

el, Pace and Inflection of **VOICE** *and* **INSTRUMENT**

NEGLIGIBLE MAINTENANCE COST

New standard of excellence in professional recording with **all-new** electronics

The Ampex Model 351 sets the highest standard in professional tape recording performance. Completely new inside, it combines the latest in circuits and electronics with Ampex superior tape handling characteristics.

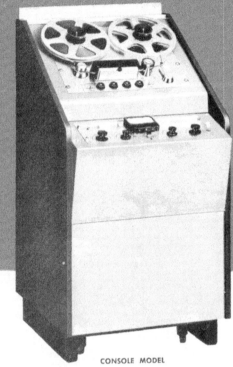

CONSOLE MODEL

NEW ETCHED CIRCUITS — The "plug-in" connections and miniature tubes give finest performance with utmost reliability and low maintenance. Completely accessible.

NEW INPUT STAGE — Lower noise level. Takes a non-critical tube.

NEW PLUS 8 OUTPUT — (600 ohms — 2 volts) Push-pull output stage matches the level of most other radio and recording equipment. Can be wired for a plus 4 output if desired.

NEW INTERNAL POWER SUPPLY — Now located on the amplifier chassis. Also makes the recorder easier to "rack." Takes up less space.

NEW "DE-POPPED" RECORDING CONTROLS — Bias build-up on recording is slower — decay is controlled when going out of recording.

ETCHED CIRCUITS

AVAILABLE WITH TWO CHANNELS! Lets you take advantage of the new techniques of mastering monaurals from multi-channel originals . . . enter the booming stereo market . . . take on special assignments. Each channel can be used separately or can be locked together.

REMOTE CONTROL UNIT

REMOTE CONTROL! You can completely control the model 351 from a distance with the optional remote control unit. Duplicates all controls including Start, Stop, Record, Fast Forward, and Rewind. Has a Red Light to indicate Record and a Green Light for Play.

An Ampex 351 spec sheet, continued on next page.

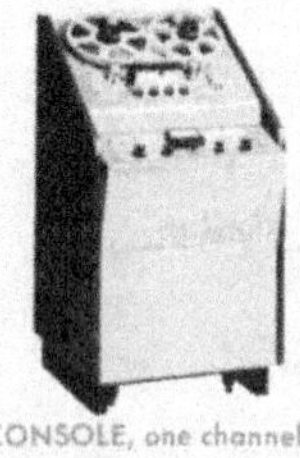

CONSOLE, one channel only   UNMOUNTED (RACK), one and two channels   PORTABLE, one and two channels

GENERAL PERFORMANCE CHARACTERISTICS AND SPECIFICATIONS

TAPE SPEEDS	7½ and 15 ips. or 3¾ and 7½ ips.
FREQUENCY RESPONSE	All versions: 15 ips. ±2 db 30 to 18,000 cps. 7½ ips. ±2 db 40 to 12,000 cps. down not more than 4 db at 30 cps and 15 kc. 3¾ ips. ±2 db 40 to 8,000 cps.

SIGNAL-TO-NOISE RATIO			
		Peak Record Level	
	Speed	to Unweighted Noise	
	15"	Full track 60 db	The peak record level is defined as that level at which the overall (input to output) total RMS. harmonic distortion is 3% when measured on a 400 cycle tone. Noise is measured when erasing a signal of peak recording level and in absence of new signal. Thus, bias and erase noise are included as well as playback amplifier noise. All components between 30 and 15,000 cycles are measured.
		Half track 55 db	
		2 Channel stereo 55 db	
	7½"	Full track 60 db	
		Half track 55 db	
		2 Channel stereo 55 db	
	3¾"	50 db	

FLUTTER AND WOW	
	15 ips. Well below 0.15% RMS. 7½ ips. Well below 0.2% RMS. 3¾ ips. Well below 0.25% RMS.

PLAYING TIMES	Speed	Half Track	Full Track
With NAB 10½"	15 ips.	64 min.	32 min.
reels (2400 feet of	7½ ips.	2 hrs. 8 min.	64 min.
tape)	3¾ ips.	4 hrs. 16 min.	2 hrs. 8 min.

STARTING TIME	Instantaneous (tape accelerates to full speed in less than 1/10 second).
STOPPING TIME	At 15 ips. speed, tape moves less than two inches after pressing "Stop" button.
PLAYBACK TIMING ACCURACY	±0.2% (±3.6 seconds in a thirty minute recording).
REWIND TIME	Approximately one minute for 2400-foot NAB reel; 30 seconds for 1200-foot EIA reel. Rewind times for thin base tapes proportionately longer.
CONTROLS	Tape motion controlled by four pushbuttons; Start, Stop, Fast Forward and Rewind. Separate Record button energizes record circuits, which drop out when machine is stopped. Individual Record button control for each channel in 2 Channel stereo machines. Motor speed and electronic equalization for various tape speeds are controlled by separate switches. Reel Size Switch provides proper tape tensions for NAB 10½" reels or EIA 5" and 7" reels.
RECORD INPUT	A switch allows recorder to accommodate either microphone input or to bridge a 600 ohm line, balanced or unbalanced. Minimum input signal for recommended record level is — 10 dbm balanced bridge, or — 13 dbm unbalanced bridge. Levels as low as 150 microvolts at the microphone input will produce the recommended record level.
PLAYBACK OUTPUT	Plus 8 dbm output into 600 ohms, balanced or unbalanced. Will feed a high input impedance amplifier directly with approximately two volts. Can be connected for +4 dbm by restrapping.
AMPLIFIERS	Separate record and playback amplifiers are used. Amplifier distortion at any operating level is negligible compared to tape distortion, even when using new high-output tapes.
PLUG-IN HEAD HOUSING	Erase, record and playback heads are contained in a single plug-in head housing.
MONITORING	Independent record and playback systems allow tape to be monitored while recording. A phone jack is provided to monitor either the record input signal before or during recording, or the output signal from the playback head while recording or during playback. An A-B switch is incorporated in order that direct comparison can be made between the original program and the recorded program. The same switch transfers a 4-inch VU meter for level comparison and monitoring. The VU meter is also used to read bias and erase current.
POWER REQUIREMENTS	Either half or full-track machines require 2.0 amperes at 117 volts AC., 2 Channel stereo requires 2.5 amperes. Machines are available for either 50 or 60 cycle operation.
RACK SPACE	Standard 19 inch wide panel with commercial notching. Tape Transport, 15¾ inches of rack space, weight . . . 58 lbs. Electronic Assembly, 7 inches of rack space, weight . . . . 18 lbs. (Two required for 2 Channel stereo.)
CONSOLE DIMENSIONS	48 inches high x 24½ inches wide x 28½ inches deep; weight . . . 168 lbs. (crated 260 lbs.).
OPTIONS TO SPECIFY WHEN ORDERING	Mounting Style — Console, rack-mount or two case portable for Full or Half Track; rack, or portable for 2 Channel stereo. Tape Speed — 7½ and 15 ips. or 3¾ and 7½ ips. Track Configuration — Full track, or half track, or 2 track stereo. Power Line Frequency — 60 or 50 cps. (117 V. only).

REMOTE CONTROL UNITS	Catalog No. 5763-2 and Catalog No. 5763-3. Controls Start, Stop, Fast Forward, Rewind and Record from a remote location. Catalog No. 5763-2 is mounted in a wooden case and is completely wired. Catalog No. 5763-3 is mounted on a flat plate for flush mounting in studio consoles and is not wired.
ACCESSORIES	Standard Alignment Tape — for 15 ips. Catalog No. 4494; for 7½ ips. Catalog No. 5563; and for 3¾ ips. Catalog No. 6000. Head Demagnetizer — Catalog No. 704.

Offices and Representatives in
Principal Cities Throughout the World

Audio Products Division
AMPEX PROFESSIONAL PRODUCTS COMPANY
934 CHARTER STREET • REDWOOD CITY, CALIFORNIA

The hits just keep on coming. Advances in the 300 model series produces the Ampex 351.

Right out of 1957: Control room of Norman Petty Recording Studio, 1313 W. 7th Street, Clovis, New Mexico. Bottom, the studio building, which also housed Petty's Nor Va Jak Music. Petty produced Buddy Holly and the Crickets, Buddy Knox and the Rhythm Orchids, the Fireballs, and other acts. (Photos Courtesy of Doug Hanners, c. 1990.)

THE BEST THING YET!

Is to plan a party and include Norman Petty in your plans. He has tape recorders that make you the life of any party. You can amaze and amuse your guests by renting a tape recorder. That would be something to slip up on your friend's conversation and record it. Sounds like fun! Want to try it? Call the Norman Petty Recording Studios, Phone 365-J, Clovis. Go to 1321 West 7th. Reflections of you on film and on record are available at the Norman Petty Studios.

A venerable Magnecord, for the professional musician as well as for the home.

A King Records mastering engineer at work in the early 1950s. King was a major independent label based in Cincinnati. It brought the public Cowbody Copas, Hawkshaw Hawkins, Grandpa Jones, the Delmore Brothers, and many other seminal country acts, whose records were usually recorded And mastered at King's recording studios. King also recorded James Brown and other big R&B acts.

Mics! Mics! Mic! And by the mid-1950s, Electro-Voice made a number of different types.

Here a man goes on location to capture nature's sounds with an Ampex.
Oh, the simplicity of the mid- to late-1950s.

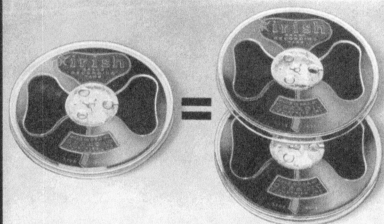

*By 1956, Irish tape had become a major brand, and tape
in general was growing along with vinyl records.*

ALBERT PULLEY, *Chief Recording Engineer, RCA Victor Record Division*

Photo by *Arnold Newman*

" 'SCOTCH' Brand High Output Tape meets <u>all</u> our demands for RCA Stereophonic recordings!"

ALBERT PULLEY, *Chief Recording Engineer,* RCA Victor Record Division, holds an enviable position in the field of audio engineering. His contributions to the development of high fidelity sound over a period of years have helped establish the United States as a leader in recorded sound. In addition, his brilliant and sensitive supervision of recordings by such masters as Toscanini, Stokowski and Koussevitsky have won him the warm praise of critics and technicians alike.

To meet the exacting standards demanded for RCA Victor "Red Seal" Stereophonic recordings requires the finest recording material available. That is why RCA uses new "Scotch" Brand No. 120A High Output Tape for their original recordings. With no increase in noise or harmonic distortion . . . 133% more output, new "Scotch" Brand No. 120A High Output Tape assures audio engineers clearer, greater dynamic range recordings. Have you tried it?

Reg. U.S. Pat. Off.

SCOTCH Magnetic Tapes
BRAND

The term "SCOTCH" and the plaid design are registered trademarks for Magnetic Tape made in U.S.A. by MINNESOTA MINING AND MFG. CO., St. Paul 6, Minn. Export Sales Office: 99 Park Avenue, New York 17, N. Y. In Canada: Minnesota Mining and Manufacturing of Canada, Ltd., P.O. Box 757, London, Ontario.

Scotch brand tape teamed with RCA Records in the mid-1950s. Here, the chief RCA recording engineer stands behind a one track tape recorder.

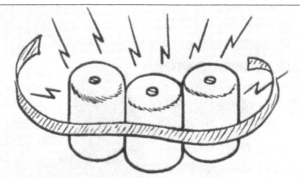

English tape deck heads were available in the States in the 1950s.

C. W. Smiley, president and Dr. Hans Wolf, musical director of Livingston Electronics listen to a binaural master tape. Dr. Wolf follows the score for correctness of musical interpretation while Mr. Smiley holds the stop watch on the tape.

Livingston engineers researching binaural system, c. 1955.

(Courtesy Hi-Fi Tape Recording)

The early recorders came equipped with tubes, not transistors. From the mid-1950s.

Presto made its name in the era of disc-cutting for masters. By the early 1950s, the firm was making tape recorders, too. The future was in magnetic recording.

SPECIFICATIONS

TYPE RC-7 MECHANISM

Reels: 7" RMA
Record speeds: Standard: 7½" and 15"/sec.
Fast Speed: 250" sec. Rewind and forward.
Frequency Response:
  50-15,000 at 15"/sec.
  50-10,000 at 7½"/sec.
Dynamic range: Better than 50 db at 3% RMS distortion.
Instantaneous Speed Accuracy: 0.15% at 15"/sec. or better, 0.20% at 7½"/sec. or better.
Power Required: 115 volts, 60 cycle, single phase, 110 watts.
Weight: 40 lbs.
Controls: Rotary Switch.
Dimensions in Case: 16"x11¼"x14".
Rack Mounting: 19"x14".

TYPE 900-A2 AMPLIFIER

Composition: One recording amplifier, one monitoring amplifier, power supply.
Response: 50-15,000 cps.
Input facilities: 3 Microphones — 1 line (bridging).
Output facilities: 500 ohm at 28dbm or 500 at +8dbm for line.
Equalization: As required for Presto tape recorder heads.
Tube Complement: Same for both recording and monitoring sections: two 6J7, one 6SL7-GT and one 6SN7-GT.
Power supply: one 5Y3.
Input Impedance: Microphones—250 ohms or bridging — ½ megohm.
Output Impedance: 500 ohms.
Power Requirement: 115 volts, 60 cycles, 70 watts
Input level of recording amplifier: for low level, low impedance microphones. Bridging input: 8dbm.
Output level of monitor amplifier: 28dbm.
Panel size: Amplifier section 19"x7; power supply 19"x3½".
Dimensions: packed for shipping 22"x7"x10½" complete unit.
Weight: 47 lbs. packed for shipment.

TYPE 901-A1 AMPLIFIER

This equipment same as 900-A2 above except that microphone inputs have been substituted with balanced line input only — either high impedance bridging or 500 ohm matching.

TYPE RC-10-24 MECHANISM

Reels: 7½" RMA reel and 10½" NAB hub.
Record speeds: Standard, 7½ and 15"/sec.
Fast speeds: 250"/sec. Rewind and forward.
Frequency response: 50 to 15,000 cps at 15"/sec. 50 to 8,000 cps at 7½"/sec.
Dynamic range: 55 db at 3% RMS distortion.
Instantaneous Speed Accuracy: 0.15% at 15"/sec. or better, 0.20% at 7½"/sec. or better.
Power required: 115 volts, 60 cycle, single phase, 200 Watts.
Weight: 115 lbs. packed for shipment.
Control: Push button switch.
Panel Dimensions: 19"x24½".
Dimensions: Packed for shipment 36"x21"x13"

TYPE RC-10-14 MECHANISM

Panel Dimensions: 19"x14"
Controls: Rotary switch
(All other specifications same as RC-10/24 above.)

TYPE A-920 AMPLIFIER

Composition: One recording preamplifier, one playback preamplifier which are switched alternately to the main power amplifier, depending on whether the unit is used for recording or playback. The playback preamplifier can be used for monitoring directly from the tape while recording. Power supply is built into the unit.
Response: 50 — 15,000 cps.
Input facilities: 1 microphone — 1 line (bridging).
Output facilities: 10 watts across 15 ohms or +8 dbm at 500 ohm line output.
Equalization: As required for Presto tape recorder heads.
Tube Complement: Same for both recording and monitoring sections; two 6J7, three 6SL7-GT, two 6V6GT, one 5Y3GT.
Input Impedance: Microphone — 250 ohms impedance or bridging input .5 meg.
Output Impedance: 15 ohms or 500 ohms.
Power Requirements: 115 volts, 50/60 cycles, single phase, 110 watts.
Input level of recording amplifier: for low level, low impedance microphones. Bridging input: 8 dbm.
Output Level of Monitor amplifier: 10 watts.
Panel size: 19"x7".
Weight: 32½ lbs.

PRESTO RECORDING CORPORATION • P. O. BOX 500, HACKENSACK, NEW JERSEY

World's Greatest Manufacturer of Instantaneous Sound Recording Equipment and Discs

Page two of the Presto spec sheet, mid-1950s.

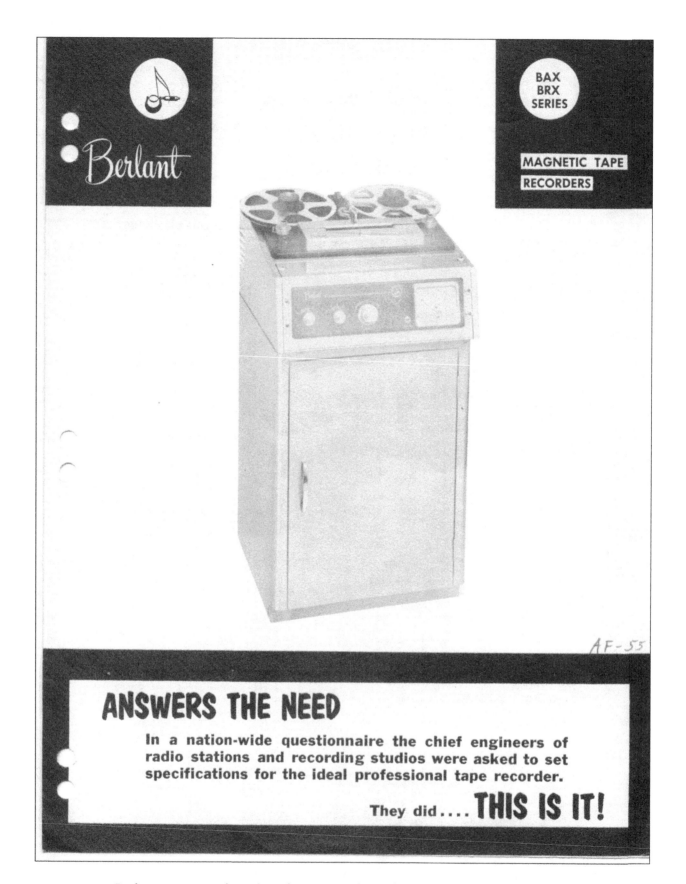

BAX
BRX
SERIES

MAGNETIC TAPE
RECORDERS

AF-55

ANSWERS THE NEED

In a nation-wide questionnaire the chief engineers of radio stations and recording studios were asked to set specifications for the ideal professional tape recorder.

They did.... **THIS IS IT!**

Berlant was an early maker of tape recorders. This studio model is from 1955.

(Effective July 1, 1955)   Professional User's Net Prices

BERLANT SERIES X RECORDERS

MODEL NO.	DESCRIPTION	USER's NET PRICE
*BRX-1	BROADCAST RECORDER: 7½ and 15 i.p.s. Complete, consisting of separate matched drive mechanism and amplifier. Two-channel input mixer. Cannon connectors. Tape motion regulator. Single track erase and record heads, dual track playback to play both single and dual track tapes..	$595.00
BRX-1-BX-SP	BROADCAST RECORDER: Same as BRX-1, except with Sync Pulse System added for exact synchronization of recorder with motion picture camera	792.50
BRX-2	BROADCAST RECORDER: Same as BRX-1, except with three dual track heads......................	595.00
*BAX-1	AUTOMATIC RECORDER: Same as BRX-1, except solenoid operated. Remote control (RCU) units extra. Single track erase and record heads, dual track playback..............................	745.00
BAX-1-BX-SP	AUTOMATIC RECORDER: Same as BAX-1, except with Sync Pulse System added for exact synchronization of recorder with motion picture camera	942.50
BAX-2	AUTOMATIC RECORDER: Same as BAX-1, except with three dual track heads......................	745.00
SBX-4	STEREO-MONAURAL RECORDER: 7½ and 15 i.p.s. Complete, consisting of separate drive mechanism and two amplifiers for 2-channel or 1-channel recording. Two half-track erase heads, "stacked" binaural record and playback heads, channel selector switch........	845.00
SBAX-4	STEREO-MONAURAL AUTOMATIC RECORDER: Same as SBX-4, except solenoid operated. Remote control (RCU) units extra...	995.00
*BRDBX-4	BROADCAST RECORDER: Same as BRX-1 except adapted for transmitting a delayed broadcast and simultaneously recording an incoming program	640.00
BRSDX-5	BROADCAST RECORDER: For single and dual operation. Five heads include BT-1, BT-22, BT-3, BT-44, and BT-66. With necessary switching and wiring	680.00
NOTE:	All recorders are suitable for installation in standard 19" relay racks, cabinets, consoles, or carrying cases as described on Accessory Sheet CA-MCM-GSA. 50 cycle drive motors can be supplied on Berlant Recorders at an additional charge of....	25.00
	Recorders with 3¾ and 7½ i.p.s. tape speeds can be supplied on a special order at an additional charge of...	25.00
	*These models available on order with full width (.200") playback heads at additional charge of	10.00

REFER TO BERLANT RECORDER ACCESSORY CATALOG SHEET FOR PRICE INFORMATION AND DESCRIPTION OF MIXERS AND OTHER ACCESSORIES.

Berlant Concertone ®

MANUFACTURERS OF CONCERTONE HIGH FIDELITY TAPE RECORDERS AND ACCESSORIES
AUDIO DIVISION—AMERICAN ELECTRONICS, INC.
4917 W. Jefferson Blvd., Los Angeles 16, California • REpublic 1-2141

LITHO IN U.S.A.   CA-BRX

Page two of the Berlant Series X spec sheet.

AUTOMATIC RECORDERS

BAX-1

BAX-2

REMOTE CONTROL

Any number of remote control stations at any distance from the recorder control all tape motion ...rations. Special RECORD SAFE-TY features prevents accidental ...sure. Recorder operates from both remote station and recorder itself in any sequence. Colored lights keep remote operator informed of recorder's functioning.

"JOY STICK" CONTROL

A distinct advancement in automatic control over the usual bank of push-buttons. A quick flick of the thumb . . . it's on "run." At any speed, another flick stops the tape. Fast forward and reverse are just as simple. A **single** automatic control lever makes operation fool-proof.

**ALL OTHER BERLANT RECORDER FEATURES ARE
STANDARD ON THE BAX SERIES.**

TO THE ENGINEER:

Compare these recorders, point by point, with any other machines on the market, regardless of price. You will find our new automatic recorders and manually operated recorders are completely versatile — designed to meet your specifications for dependable performance, economical cost and simplified maintenance.

Bert Berlant

*Page one of a promotional spec sheet is followed by page two.
The recorders are aimed at the broadcast market. Next page, more information.*

Berlant

NEW IMPROVED BRX SERIES BROADCAST RECORDERS

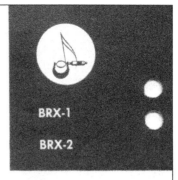

BRX-1

BRX-2

SPECIFICATIONS

TAPE SPEEDS:
Model BRX-1, BRX-2—Instantaneous selection of 15"/sec. or 7.5"/sec.
Model BRX-3S, BRX-3D—Instantaneous selection of 7.5"/sec. or 3.75"/sec.

FREQUENCY RESPONSE:
±2db from 40 to 15,000 CPS at 15"/sec.
±4db from 40 to 15,000 CPS at 7.5"/sec.
±2db from 50 to 5,000 CPS at 3.75"/sec.

SIGNAL TO NOISE RATIO:
55 db as measured by proposed NARTB standard (400 CPS at 3% T.H.D.)

TOTAL HARMONIC DISTORTION:
1% at zero V.U.

TIMING ACCURACY:
Better than 99.8%

TOTAL FLUTTER AND WOW:
Less than 0.1% RMS at 15"/sec.
Less than 0.2% RMS at 7.5"/sec.
Less than 0.3% RMS at 3.75"/sec.

REWIND AND FAST FORWARD:
Less than 60 secs. for 2,500 feet
FROM STOP TO 15"/SEC.:
0.1 second

HEAD MOUNTING:
Interchangeable Bracket mounting up to FIVE heads.

METER INDICATION:
Bias Current, Record Level, Output Level.

MONITOR OUTPUT:
From tape or input signal.

INPUT IMPEDANCE:
One megohm on high impedance microphone input. 50/250 ohms balanced or unbalanced with plug-in transformer #T-3344. 200,000 ohms unbalanced bridging input.

INPUT SENSITIVITY:
1 mv on microphone input
.06 volt on bridging input.

OUTPUT IMPEDANCE:
Cathode follower. 600 ohms balanced output with plug-in transformer #T-2560.

OUTPUT LEVEL:
6 volts from cathode follower output.
Zero DBM across 600 ohm line.

FILAMENT SUPPLY:
D.C. on all filaments.

DIMENSIONS:
Drive mechanism, 14" x 19"
6½" below panel
Amplifier, 5¼" x 19"
Mounting depth, 6" below panel.

WEIGHT:
Drive mechanism, 35 lbs.
Amplifier, 10 lbs.

TUBE LIST:
2-12AX7; 1-12AT7; 2-12AU7; 1-12BH7; 1-6X5GT

POWER REQUIRED:
160 Watts, 60 cycles, 115 volts
Special 50 cycle drive motor available. Use step-down transformer for higher line voltages.

BROADCAST RECORDER
in BRDC and BRPAC
carrying cases
$745.00 complete

By using a combination of four heads and two amplifier units, BERLANT-CONCERTONE has designed binaural versions of its tape recorders that provide a versatility of performance hitherto unknown in the recording art. Available as an automatic or manually operated unit, each of these machines can be looked upon as two independent recorders using a common reel of tape with the two channels capable of being operated either separately or in conjunction with each other.

IMPROVED HYSTERESIS SYNCHRONOUS DIRECT DRIVE MOTOR
with 99.8% timing accuracy now on all BRX Series Recorders, guarantees dependability and long-life performance.

TWO-CHANNEL INPUT MIXER
permits recording and mixing of two signals simultaneously with independent volume control on each. Microphone and line inputs for high impedance—or low impedance with plug-in transformers.

TAPE MOTION REGULATOR
Stabilizes tape motion and improves tape tension arm control.

CANNON CONNECTORS
Standard equipment on all models.

SYNC PULSE SYSTEM
For synchronizing tape with 35 or 16 mm motion picture film. Added to, or installed in any BR Recorder at extra cost, it provides perfect synchronization between recorder and camera. For studio or location use.

AB-TEST FADER
Allows monitoring between incoming signal and playback from tape without transients or clicks. Separate volume controls for RECORD and PLAYBACK permit sufficient level while monitoring to compare accurately incoming signal with recorded signal on tape.

PROVISION FOR FIVE HEADS
Eliminates a second recorder for most operations. An extra playback head and amplifier unit permits transmitting a delayed broadcast while recording and monitoring an incoming program. Add a second record and erase head for both single and dual track operation on one recorder. Sound-on-sound recording, echo chamber effects, and other special uses now possible with one recorder.

HALF TRACK PLAYBACK HEAD
Allows playback of either single or dual track tapes. Full track playback also available.

ADJUSTABLE BIAS
Permits setting bias frequency to match requirements of various tape coatings for perfection in recording.

CUEING AND EDITING
"Cue" position of lever puts tape in contact with heads and releases brakes so that reels can be rotated by hand while listening to signal. When exact cue point is reached head cover may be opened to "Edit" position for free access to tape.

- INSTANTANEOUS REELOKS
- AUTOMATIC CUT-OFF
- 4½ ILLUMINATED SIGNAL LEVER INDICATOR
- STRAIGHT LINE THREADING
- THREE MOTORS
- ERASE SAFETY

SWITCH
AND CAM SHAFT
ASSEMBLY

"45" RPM
TONE ARM

CLUTCH
ASSEMBLY

"BRAKE ARM"
ASSEMBLY

MICROSWITCH

COUPLINGS

The new RCA 45 RPM Conversion Kit, MI-11883—installed. The kit is complete with (a) clutch assembly (speed changer); (b) brake-arm assembly; (c) switch and cam shaft assembly; (d) microswitch; (e) dial plate; (f) shaft coupling; and (g) adapter hub.

The fine-groove tone arm and pick-up for "45 RPM" are available extra.

Play 45 RPM's on 70-series Turntables—
with RCA Kit MI-11883

NOW you can handle 45's, 78's or 33-1/3's—fine-groove or standard —with this kit, and a second tone arm (available extra).

Easy to install

You install the single-unit, ball-type speed reducer between the two flexible couplings in the main drive shaft of your turntable. You transfer the motor switch leads to the micro-switch—included with the kit. That's all there is.

Easy to operate

A motor-control knob on the deck of the turntable controls the speed. Position No. 1 stops the motor. No. 2 shifts the speed control to the 78-33 ½

rpm speed-change lever (on turntable deck). No. 3 shifts to "45 rpm" position (speed lever set at 78 rpm). *You can shift speeds instantly in either direction while turntable is running.*

Same RCA broadcast dependability

Sturdy construction and accurate mechanical alignment assures you the same quiet, trouble-free service for which more than five thousand RCA turntables are famous.

*As tape recording was hitting big in 1949,
RCA developed a heavy-duty turntable for radio
and recording studios.*

PUSH-BUTTONS

ELECTRICALLY INTERLOCKED USING 7 D. C. RELAYS AND 1 SOLENOID

THREE HEADS, PROFESSIONAL TYPE RECORDER, AMPLIFIERS, 4″ VU METER
AND 8″ EXTENDED RANGE SPEAKER IN PORTABLE CASE WITH 2 COVERS.

SIZE: 16″x23″x11″
Weight: 62 pounds

TAPESONIC

$368⁵⁰
NET PRICE

RECORDER MODEL 70-B

1. Monitoring from tape while recording, three separate heads. A. B. switch permits comparison between original and recorded program.

2. 3 speeds, 15″, 7½″ and 3¾″/Sec.

3. Fast forward and rewind, 1 minute for 2500 ft. NARTB reel.

4. Large 4″ VU meter for recording level.

5. 3 heavy duty dynamically balanced motors.

6. Dual track, will play 4 hours at 3¾″.

7. Push pull 12 watts 10 tubes, power, record, playback, mixers and monitor amplifiers. D. C. on preamplier filaments.

8. High fidelity, 40 - 16,000 cycles ± 3db at 15″, 40 - 13,000 cycles ± 3 db at 7½″ and 40 - 6,500 cycles ± 3 db at 3¾″.

9. Low flutter and wow, .1% at 15″, .2% at 7½″ and .3% at 3¾″.

10. Separate bass and treble controls.

11. Mixing channels for microphone, radio or phono inputs.

12. Drive mechanism is mounted on a rigid aluminum casting.

13. Electro dynamic brake action and tape tension, never requires adjustment.

14. Signal to noise ratio 55 db. above tape hiss level.

PREMIER ELECTRONIC LABORATORIES   382 LAFAYETTE ST., NEW YORK 3, N. Y.

*The Tapesonic was another professional tape recorder capable of running at 15 IPS.
This spec sheet was distributed to dealers in 1955.*

Need a little instruction on recording? Early 1950s.

Discs made from "SCOTCH" Magnetic Tape masters earn Capitol's Full Dimensional Sound Seal!

Capitol Record's Full Dimensional Sound Review Committee. Left to right: Bob Myers; Roy Du Nann, Supervising Recording Engineer; Ed Uecke, Chief Electronics Engineer; Bill Miller and Francis Scott of the Capitol Artists and Repertoire Department.

You can thank the critical judgment of the five men pictured above for the wonderful tone and fidelity of the Capitol records you buy. They have the responsibility of listening to *every* Capitol Classical LP master recording before it is released to the public . . . appraising each disc's dynamic range, performance, background noise— in fact, judging it on *eight* critical points. Only the recordings which meet all of this Committee's rigid standards receive Capitol Record's famous gold stamp-of-quality . . . the Full Dimensional Sound Seal.

Capitol Record's Full Dimensional Sound Review Committee is *unique* in the recording field. But the mag-netic tape the company uses for its original recordings is the same favored by *all* leading record firms—"SCOTCH" Magnetic Recording Tape. Only "SCOTCH" Brand makes its own magnetic coat-ings. This means *all* mag-netic particles are alive, active — ready to record even the faintest sound with perfect fidelity. No wonder it's the largest-selling magnetic tape *in the world!*

In 1956, Scotch again connected with a major company, Capitol Records. Here is Capitol's "Full Dimensional Sound Review Committee," which includes the company's chief engineer and an A&R representative. Note a recorder behind them on the left and a turntable on the right.

Radio personality Martin Block stands at the recorder in the 1950s to promote Mylar, the polyester tape.

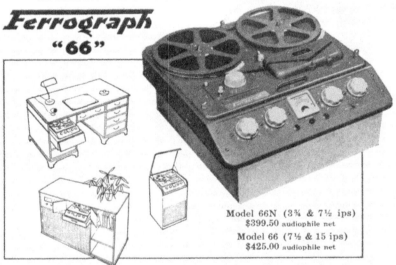

*By the mid-1950s, Ercona, a New York firm,
had entered the U.S. recorder market.*

Designed for making
Modern High Fidelity
Recordings

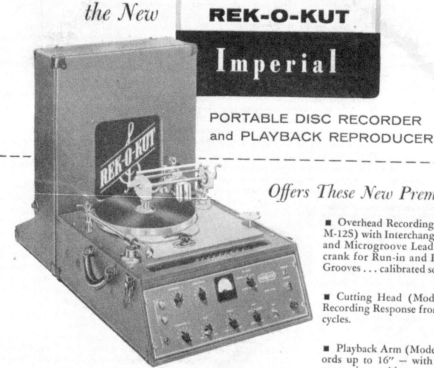

the New **REK-O-KUT**

Imperial

PORTABLE DISC RECORDER
and PLAYBACK REPRODUCER

Offers These New Premium Features:

■ Overhead Recording Lathe (Model M-12S) with Interchangeable Standard and Microgroove Leadscrews. Hand-crank for Run-in and Run-off Spiral Grooves . . . calibrated scale for timing.

■ Cutting Head (Model R-56) with Recording Response from 50 to 10,000 cycles.

■ Playback Arm (Model 160) for records up to 16" — with dual-sapphire magnetic cartridge.

The new Rek-O-Kut Imperial is equipped with a Model TR-12H Turntable driven by a hysteresis motor. Recording and playback amplifier is built-in. Recordings can be made from tape, live, 'off-the-air' or from other record discs — at 33⅓ and 78 rpm (45 rpm optional).

Imperial

complete with Cutting Head, 120-line Leadscrew and Timing Chart $599⁹⁵*

(less microphone)

*slightly higher West of Rockies

New Model M-12S
Overhead Recording Lathe
fits Rek-O-Kut Challenger Disc Recorders
available separately.

with 120-line Leadscrew
and Timing Chart
(less Cutting Head) $150⁰⁰*
Model R-56 Cutting Head............ 60⁰⁰

(Interchangeable Leadscrew Prices — available on request)

See your sound dealer — or write to Dept. VE-24

REK-O-KUT COMPANY, 38-01 Queens Blvd., Long Island City 1, N. Y.
EXPORT: Morhan Exporting Corp., 458 Broadway, New York 13, N.Y.
CANADA: Atlas Radio Corp., 50 Wingold Ave., Toronto 10, Ontario

In 1953, Rek-O-Kut was one of the top makers of disc recorders, but audio engineers found tape recordings more to their liking. They were easy to edit.

er professional mikes, this unit has a switch, making selection of several low-impedances possible.

Both the ribbon and dynamic mike of high quality exhibit most excellent frequency response, many being flat within the customary few db from 30 to 15,000 cycles. There are claims that the ribbon is apt to be of somewhat higher sensitivity than the dynamic, due to its inherent low mass of moving parts, but good quality dynamics are most amazing in their sensitivity. In general, the ribbon and dynamic low-impedance microphones exhibit vastly improved response over the crystal microphone, or ceramic unit, although we hasten to advise, that some forms of crystal microphone can be made into strong competitors. The objection to hum, and line loss with crystal mikes, is handled by built-in impedance step-down transformers, which convert the high-impedance output to low-impedance for the cables, the reverse being used to step it back up to a useful impedance for our tape recorder input.

An examination of the instruction book for your tape unit will show if you have a low-impedance input available, or if you must use an input transformer.

Another significant consideration in selecting a microphone is pick-up pattern. Generally mikes fall into three groups, uni-directional, picking up sound from one direction only, bi-directional, from two directions, and omni-directional, from all directions. There are variations of shape of pattern, such as the "cardioid," etc., but these are of little consequence.

What pattern is best for you depends on what type of recording you will be doing. If you record at concerts, etc., where a crowd is present, and usually noisy, avoid the omni-directional mike like the plague, and look twice before going for a bi-directional type. If this is your meat, stick to the uni-directional mike, or the omni-directional capable of

Left: Fentone Blue Ribbon mike, a 50 ohm velocity unit, made by Band and Olufsen in Denmark. Notice the tiny transformer below the magnet, which raises the ribbon impedance to 50 ohms. Right: Shure 333 velocity microphone, a ribbon mike with uni-directional pick-up pattern. This unit features three impedances, controlled by built-in switch.

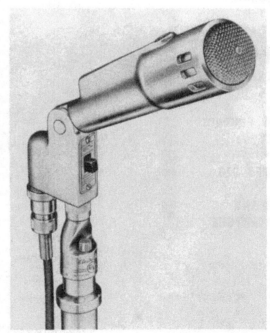

The Electro-Voice 664, a quality dynamic microphone. The author's experience shows this microphone to come close in performance to the best broadcast dynamics.

tissue thin ribbon of aluminum, which flexes with air velocity in a strong magnetic field, being all the wire for the coil. It is also called "velocity" mike since it is controlled by air velocity, not pressure. To the writer's knowledge, all contain a transformer, needed to raise the level up to even the common low-impedance levels of 50 or 150 ohms. The ribbon mike has an impedance at the source, of a fraction of an ohm. Most ribbon microphones are bi-directional, that is they pick up sound from both sides of the mike, often an advantage, but sometimes a disadvantage; it depends on the particular recording situation. An exception to this rule is the ingenious Shure 333, a professional ribbon mike featuring a uni-directional, or one-way pickup. Like many oth-

A couple of mid-1950s mics, Shure and Electro-Voice.

MAGNETIC FILM &
TAPE RECORDING

TONY SCHWARTZ
MASTER
RECORDIST

HOW TO AVOID
HUM

CAPTURING
YESTERDAY'S
MUSIC

BUILD THIS
RECORDING
CENTER

PUTTING A
THESIS ON TAPE

NEW PRODUCT
REPORT:

AMPEX 620

BERLANT
CONCERTONE

Tony Schwartz recording at home.

JUNE, 1955

35¢

Tony Schwartz was one of the nation's most well-known home "recordists" of the 1950s.

NEW PRODUCT REPORT

STAFF **OK** TESTED

Product: Ampex 620 Power Amplifier and Speaker
Manufacturer: Ampex Corporation, 934 Chartor Street, Redwood City, Calif.
Price: $149.50

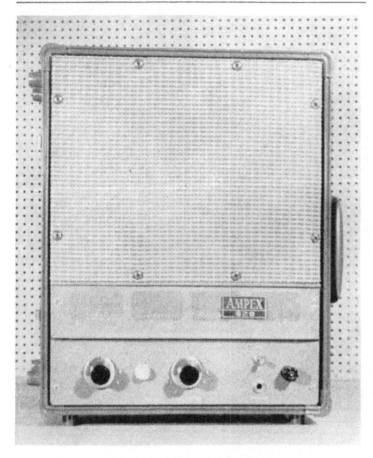

AMPEX AMPLIFIER-SPEAKER

. . . 10 watt amplifier, excellent response, characteristic of this portable unit.

THERE is an old saying that "good goods often come in small packages." That old saw is fully borne out by this amplifier - speaker combination manufactured by the Ampex Corporation.

The Ampex 620 amplifier-speaker is a companion piece to the well known Ampex 600 portable recorder. It is housed in a Samsonite luggage case of about the same dimensions as the recorder and is much the same in outward appearance.

The lid is detachable and contains loops to hold the power and audio connecting cords. The speaker is covered by an attractive grille and below the speaker grille can be found the controls. The volume control is on the left, next is an "on" indicator light and beside this the bass-treble control. An on-off switch is provided as well as a fuse receptacle and speaker outlet jack on the face of the panel.

The power and audio inputs are in a recessed well in the side of the case.

As an amplifier-speaker combination, excellent results were obtained on test. The frequency response measure with the unit at 2 watts output into its nominal impedance was 30 to 15,000 cycles per second at less than 1 dbm linear attenuation from a reference point of 1000 cycles per second. It had less than

1% audio distortion, which is quite remarkable considering the circuit which is used. This is a three stage push-pull output having phase inverted drivers and a high-gain voltage amplifier. We noted several equalizing and reciprocal networks, some of which are directly associated with the speaker input.

The fine results we obtained are the more remarkable as the speaker unit is a single cone permanent magnet type. This is housed in an enclosure damped by a thick blanket of what appears to be Fiberglas. The packing prevents resonances and the success of this method is attested by the fact that our tests indicated an excellent reponse with but minor deviations up to more than 10,-000 cycles and good flatness of response down to 50 cycles per second. This exceeds the claims made by the manufacturer.

Many novel arrangements have been incorporated into the speaker with the net result that reproduction is excellent to about 8 watts output—which is more than enough for the average room.

The tone compensation is a single control with the zero positon at the center for a flat response.

A maximum of 8 dbm of bass gain is to be had with the control all the way in the bass position and on the high side a gain of 6 dbm is indicated at 10,000 cycles.

The input to the amplifier-speaker is high impedance and it will accommodate such things as a record player or

The 620 is housed in a mar resistant Samsonite luggage type case that matches the model 600 portable Ampex recorder.

An Ampex amplifier-speaker, 1955.

Now...record the whole performance...
without a break!

Got a favorite concert or opera program you'd like to preserve on tape? Symphony or dramatic production? Now, *record it all* using new "Scotch" Brand Extra Play Magnetic Tape. With 50% more tape wound on each reel, Extra Play Tape gives you as much recording time as 1½ reels of standard tape, plus strength to spare. This means annoying interruptions for reel change are sharply reduced to offer more perfect recording results.

You'll notice a crisper tone and higher fidelity, too—the result of "Scotch" Brand's exclusive oxide dispersion process. By packing minute, fine-grain oxide particles into a neater, thinner pattern, "Scotch" Brand has been able to produce a super-sensitive, high-potency magnetic recording surface. Hear the difference yourself. Try new "Scotch" Brand Extra Play Tape on your own machine.

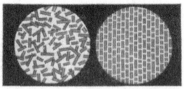

Electron Photo Microscope Shows the Difference!
At left, artist's conception of magnified view of old-fashioned oxide coating still used by most ordinary long play tapes. At right, "Scotch" Brand's new dispersion method lays fine-grain particles in an orderly pattern to give a super-sensitive recording surface that contains as much oxide as conventional tapes, yet is 50% thinner.

REG. U S. PAT. OFF.
NEW! SCOTCH BRAND
Extra Play Magnetic Tape 190

The term "SCOTCH" and the plaid design are registered trademarks for Magnetic Tape made in U.S.A. by MINNESOTA MINING AND MFG. CO., St. Paul 6, Minn. Export Sales Office: 99 Park Avenue, New York 16, N. Y. In Canada: Minnesota Mining and Manufacturing Co. of Canada, Ltd., P.O. Box 757, London, Ontario.

Scotch goes "atomic," mid-1950s.

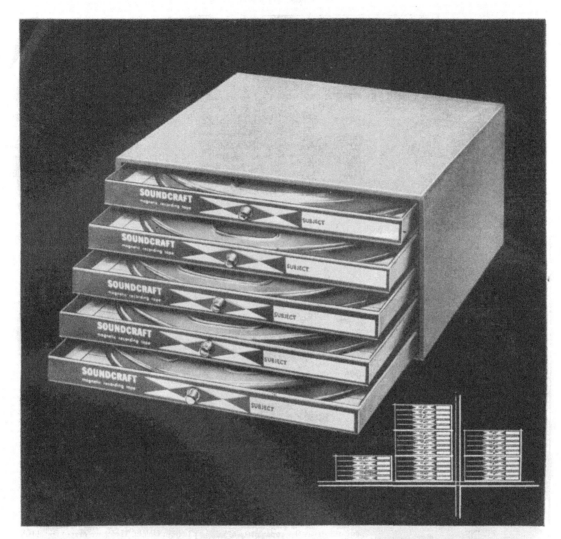

Soundcraft came up with an interesting—and handy—storage unit in the late 1950s.

Design Of A Professional Tape Recorder

WILLIAM F. BOYLAN* and WILLIAM E. GOLDSTANDT**

Design and operational features of a new high-quality machine.

THE PRESENT STATE of the magnetic recording art has made possible the design of recording equipment with extremely high performance standards—excellent frequency response, low distortion and flutter—and so on. While performance standards are of the greatest importance, a survey of individuals and requirements in the professional recording field made it plain that certain purely operational features were very much in demand as well, such as ease of tape handling, precise and instant control of tape motion, good editing facilities, accurate timing, portability, and other similar points.

These factors were taken into prime consideration in the design of the new tape recorder pictured in *Fig.* 1. In addition to fulfilling the high performance standards required in quality professional work, the machine provides extremely quick and easy operation. It consists of two major units, the tape transport and the record-reproduce amplifier unit which includes the high-frequency oscillator Both major assemblies may be mounted in the console as shown, in a portable carrying case which is furnished, or in a standard 19-inch relay rack.

Tape Transport Unit

The complete tape transport, shown in *Fig.* 2, is constructed on a standard 19-inch rack-mounting panel. The panel is 12½ inches high and the mechanism extends 8 inches behind the panel.

One of the principal design objectives for this project was to produce a mechanism which would afford easy operation and tape handling. In order to accomplish this, considerable effort was directed to the problem of panel layout. Among the people interviewed, the general trend of opinion indicated that the normal tape direction should be from left to right in both relay rack and console mounted machines. This arrangement dictated a front panel 19 inches wide with the height of the panel kept to a minimum to preserve portability.

In any professional recorder certain minimum components should be included in the panel layout. These are a constant-speed capstan and pressure roller assembly, a tape tensioning or hold-back device, a take-up system to spool the tape after it passes the capstan, erase,

record, and reproduce heads, compliance arms, and an inertia-stabilizing roller to filter out tape speed irregularities produced as the tape leaves the pay-off reel. The layout of these components not only governs the performance of the unit to a great extent, but also affects the simplicity of operation. In the machine being described the tape path is straightforward and free of loops and curves around guiderollers.

A 3-position function control lever is included. Its positions are marked OPERATE, LOAD, and EDIT. When the lever is placed in the LOAD position the compliance arms, tape guide, and head covers are put in such a position that "straightline" or "slot" loading of the tape is permitted. This feature eliminates most of the inconvenience normally encountered in tape threading. The head covers are

open wide in the LOAD position for ease of head inspection and marking of tape.

After the machine has been loaded with tape, the control lever is placed in the OPERATE position. This brings the compliance arms and head cover back into their normal positions. In the OPERATE position, the tape does not come into contact with the heads except during normal forward operation. This allows the tape to be run at high speed forward or rewind without excessive wear on the heads. When the tape is moving in the normal forward direction, as for playback or record, the tape guide and head cover are solenoid-actuated to cause the tape to engage the heads.

When the control knob is placed in the EDIT position the pushbutton switches are locked out of the circuit, and the tape is held against the heads. If one

Fig. 1. The new Magnecord M-80 recorder in its console cabinet. A portable case is also provided.

*Assistant Chief Engineer and **Mechanical Engineer, Magnecord, Inc., 225 West Ohio Street, Chicago 10, Ill.*

Tech stuff for audio engineers in the middle 1950s, when Magnecord was hot.

English record producer Joe Meek rummages through his rubble of tapes, searching perhaps for the "Telstar" mix-down master, a No. 1 record by the Tornados in America and the UK in 1962.

Take Cover!

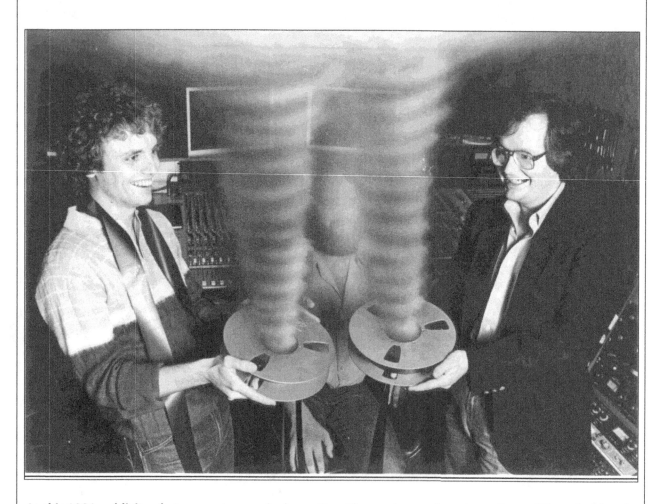

In this 1981 publicity photo, country-music singer Don King and record producer Steve Gibson hold reels of multitrack tapes that appear to have funnel clouds blowing from them. From behind, audio engineer Ron Schirmer observes. The name of King's new single? "Whirlwind," of course.

...The M80 Series

THE COMPLETE CONSOLE — M80-ACC

*The Magnecorder console model
M80-ACC is the most convenient console
on the professional market
today. Reels, heads and amplifier are
placed in perfect operating position.
Unique is the tip-out arrangement
that permits easy access to the
components for simple
maintenance and servicing.*

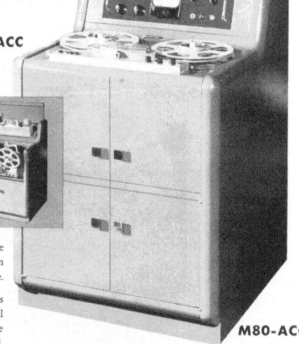

M80-ACC

coupled cascode input stages produce maximum signal-to-noise ratio and minimize hum, noise and microphonics inherent in amplifiers. Only the Magnecord M80 has the Audio Cascode.

Timing accuracy of better than 3 seconds in 30 minutes is assured through direct tape drive in conjunction with electrical supply and take-up tensioning. Integrated design produces the lowest flutter rate of any professional recorder. Differential, band brakes of stainless steel eliminate entirely the danger of thrown tape loops, grabbing or chattering. The brakes operate only to stop the tape transport. Easily interchangeable head assemblies provide for full track, half track, or instrumentation heads without loss of head alignment. Snap-mounted covers protect the head assembly during normal operation and provide for quick access for editing, cleaning and alignment. Unitized assemblies permit maximum flexibility and minimize maintenance problems. A High-Level Mixer is available for all M80 equipment, either for rack mounting or installation in the portable case.

Standard 10½ inch reels may be used on all M80 models, which give 32 minutes of play at 15"/second and 64 minutes at 7.5"/second. A switch on the front panel assures proper tension for any reel size.

New remote control box allows you to completely control your M80 equipment from any place in the studio.

RECORD AMPLIFIER SPECIFICATIONS

INPUT LEVELS: **Microphone:** −90 dbm to −30 dbm.
  Bridge, balanced: +10 dbm to −30 dbm.
  Bridge, unbalanced: Sensitivity 15 millivolts for 0 level recording.

Input impedance: Microphone, 50/150/200, balanced or unbalanced.

Noise: Equivalent input noise, Microphone Channel, −125dbm.

Pre-emphasis: 8db at 15Kc at 15"/sec. 13db at 15Kc at 7.5"/sec.

PLAYBACK AMPLIFIER SPECIFICATIONS

Output Level: +16dbm at 1.0% distortion.

Noise: 66db below a 1000 cps signal played back from a standard tape recorded at the 3% third harmonic distortion point.

Distortion: .53% with a +6dbm output at 400 cps. 1.3% with a +18dbm output at 400 cps.

Output impedance: 600 ohms, balanced or unbalanced.

Note: The M80-C amplifier has a feedback stabilized output which maintains constant output from no-load to full-load conditions. Therefore, the amplifier may be used with or without termination. Meter calibration is not affected by changes in output loading.

Metering: Bias, Record level, and Playback level are measured on a standard 4" illuminated VU meter.

Tubes: (2) 6BK7; (2) 12AU7; (1) 5Y3GT; (1) 12AX7; (1)(12BH7 oscillator on M-80-A).

Power: 72 watts at 117 volts, 60 cps

5

Magnecorders! The esteemed line shows its stuff in this 1950s multi-page spec sheet for dealers.

WHEN YOUR JOB CALLS FOR

THE HIGHEST PROFESSIONAL QUALITY

PERFECT PORTABILITY — THE M80-AC

The Magnecorder M80-AC offers for the first time a completely portable professional quality unit with such valuable features as slot loading, push button controls, automatic tape lifter and special low-noise amplifier.

M80-AC

OVERALL SPECIFICATIONS

Tape Speed: 7.5 and 15 inches per second.

Starting Time: Less than 0.1 second.

Stopping Time: Less than 2 inches of tape when operating at 15 inches per second.

Timing Accuracy: Better than ±3 seconds in 30 minutes.

Flutter and Wow: Less than 0.1% RMS Maximum at 15"/second. Less than 0.15% RMS Maximum at 7.5"/second. All Components measured 0 to 300 cps using a 3000 cps signal.

Rewind and HI-FWD Time: Less than 45 seconds for 10½ inch reels.

Playing Time: 32 minutes at 15"/sec., 64 minutes at 7.5"/sec. on 10½ inch reel.

Frequency Response: 30 to 20,000 cps ±4db, 15"/sec.; 30 to 15,000 cps ±2db, 15"/sec.; 30 to 15,000 cps ±4db, 7.5"/sec.; 50 to 10,000 cps ±2db, 7.5"/sec.

Signal-to-Noise Ratio: 58 db at both 7.5 and 15 inches per second. (Based upon 3% total harmonic distortion at 400 cps, and measuring all noise components between 30 and 15,000 cps.)

Monitoring: Phone jack on amplifier panel for head phone monitoring.

Power: 275 watts at 117 volts, 60 cps.

Panel Size: M80-A tape transport: 19" x 12¼" M80-C amplifier: 19" x 5¼"

Unit Depth: M80-A tape transport: 8½" M80-C amplifier: 8½"

Weight: M80-A tape transport: 50 lbs. M80-C amplifiers: 15 lbs.

The Magnecorder M80 incorporates the very latest advances in fine recording techniques. It may be operated at either 7.5 or 15 inches per second with a starting time of less than 1/10 second and it stops within two inches of tape travel at 15 inches per second. Proper equalization for either speed is provided by a panel switch on the amplifier. Quick slot loading and interlocking push-button controls permit instantaneous selection of desired operation with safety and reliability. The tape is automatically lifted from the heads during rewind and "high-forward" to reduce head wear to a minimum. Direct-

3 channel, high level mixer for 50/150/200 ohm microphones.

Remote Control Adaptor and Control Station Available.

See page 10 for specifications. Magnecordette models are shown in Catalog HF100.

Monitor direct from the tape
with the PT63-AH

Three heads — erase, record, playback — completely shielded to prevent cross-talk and hum — permit monitoring directly from the tape during recording. The PT63-AH was developed from the PT6 and includes all of the original features PLUS direct tape monitoring. The PT63-AHX is supplied without the case and may be easily rack mounted by use of the PT6-H adapter panel. All standard heads, including dual track can be supplied.

The PT63-AH is a completely versatile recording unit — light enough for easy portability but with quality equal to the best in permanent studio installations. Through the use of the PT63-HT throw-over switch two PT63-AH mechanisms and a single amplifier may be set up for continuous recording. Also available for this unit is a two speed hysteresis sychronous motor permitting recording at all three standard speeds (3¾", 7½" and 15" per second), or a low speed motor for 7½" and 3¾" only.

An outstanding feature of the PT6 and PT63 series of Magnecorders is the unitized construction which simplifies maintenance and permits many special and unusual equipment combinations to be made up from standard units.

PT63-AH

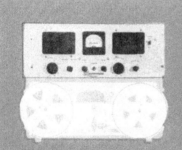

PT63-J has separate record and playback amplifiers. Features include 10 watts of audio output which may be used with external speaker or separately controlled integral speaker. Balanced 600 ohm zero level line output in addition to speaker connections. Illuminated VU may be switched to read record level, playback output level, or bias. Dual speed equalization and monitor jack for earphones. Low impedance microphone input and bridge input. May be used in portable case or rack mounted.

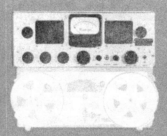

PT7-P record/playback amplifier has all of the features of the PT63-J shown at left. In addition, has three microphone inputs with high level mixing. This unit features 20-step, silver contact, mixing controls in addition to master gain control. Bridge input may be either balanced or unbalanced. Large 4 inch VU reduces operator eye strain. Supplementing the 10 watts of audio output, this amplifier has 600 ohm balanced line outputs on both record and playback amplifiers, permitting it to be used as a broadcast remote amplifier. 19 inch front panel width permits portable case or direct rack mounting.

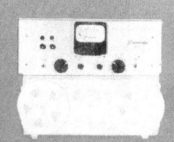

PT7-C record/playback amplifier for use in studio installations feature 600 ohm and bridge inputs either of which may be balanced or unbalanced. Large 4 inch VU permits accurate monitoring; meter may be switched to read record level, playback level, or bias. 600 ohm balanced or unbalanced zero level output is equipped with line pad to minimize effect of impedance irregularities. Dual speed recording equalization. Designed primarily for rack mounting, but portable case is available.

See page 10 for specifications. Magnecordette models are shown in Catalog HF100.

The PT6 sets the professional standard

The Magnecorder PT6-AH Basic Recorder Mechanism has long been recognized as the outstanding value in the professional field. Its high performance has become the standard of the professional recording industry.

Separate erase and record/play heads, along with capstans and pressure rollers for both 7½" and 15" tape speeds are used on the PT6-AH. Seven inch reels are standard with adapter arms for 10½" reels available as an accessory. Rewinding is fast and positive; 1200 feet in 40 seconds. "High speed" forward permits fast cueing and editing. The PT6-AH, normally case mounted, is easily rack-mounted with a PT6-H adapter panel. This professional portable recorder mechanism weighs less than 30 lbs. in its black leatherette case.

Order model PT6-AHX if no case is necessary. Full track heads are standard; half track heads may be specified. This unit is available with a 2-speed motor which permits instantaneous electrical speed change and operation at 3¾", 7½" and 15" per second. A low speed motor to permit operation at 7½" and 3¾" per second only may be ordered.

The Magnecorder PT6-AH Basic Recorder combines with any one of the amplifiers illustrated to the right.

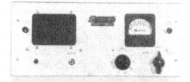

PT6-J all-purpose record/reproduce amplifier for recording from a single microphone. Low impedance mike input plus bridging input. Illuminated VU meter. 10 watts of audio output may be used with internal monitor speaker or external speakers. Amplifier also has 600 ohm balanced line output. May be used as broadcast remote amplifier. Available in compact portable carrying case or with adaptor for rack mounting.

The PT6-G is a complete recording amplifier. It has high impedance microphone, and high impedance phono or tuner inputs. Three-speed equalization for recording and playback. Eye tube for controlling recording level. Two high impedance outputs, high and low level, permit easy connection to any high fidelity system, power amplifier, radio or public address system. Monitor jack on front panel for earphones.

PT6-AH

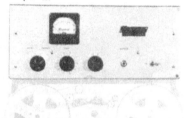

The PT6-V amplifier is a compact, but truly professional unit. Among the features are dual speed equalization, balanced low impedance microphone input and high impedance bridge input. Illuminated VU meter, and balanced or unbalanced 600 ohm output. Monitor jack for earphones. Normally supplied as part of Voyager single-case portable unit, but may be rack mounted with adaptor plates.

The Voyager PT6-VAH is a professional quality portable recorder combining in a single case the PT6-AH recorder mechanism with a PT6-V amplifier. This is an ideal light-weight unit for recording away from the studio or in the laboratory. For quick set-up, cables between recorder and amplifier are permanently plugged-in. Unit may be set-up either as illustrated or side by side.

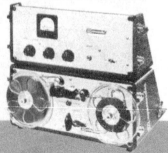

See page 10 for specifications. Magnecordette models are shown in Catalog HF100.

6

ACCESSORIES AND MODIFICATION KITS

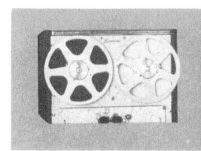 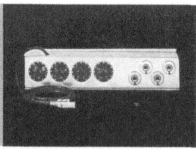 

PT6-M Auxiliary Spooling Mechanism doubles record and playback time of PT6 and 63 units. Permits use of 10½" NAB reels. 19" wide x 10½" high. May be rack mounted or used in portable case with mechanical unit. Separate rewind and take-up motors. Reels not included.

PT6-IM3 Three Channel Input Mixer (Low-level) 30/50 ohm microphones. **PT6-IM4 Four Channel Input Mixer** (Low-level) 30/50 ohm microphones. Both 17" long for portable case mounting. Either of the above may be used with PT6-J, PT63-J, and PT7-P amplifier.

PT6-S Portable Power Supply 117v 60 cycle AC from 12v DC self-contained battery, generator, frequency meter and frequency control. Runs any PT6 or 63 set for 1 hour.

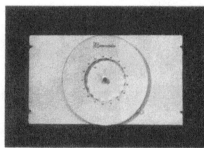 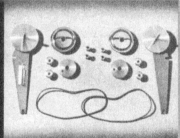 

PT6-EL Continuous Loop Mechanism. Holds up to 600 feet tape (15 minutes at 7½" per second); eliminates rewinding. 19" x 10½" for rack mounting or portable case. Used with PT6-A and PT63-A units.

93 X 4 Reel Extension Arms to adapt PT6-AH and PT63-AH to accommodate 10½" NAB reels, consists of pair of arms, plastic drive belts, and adapter hubs.

91 X 279 Voice Operated Relay plugs-in between PT6-J and PT6-AH units. Adaptable to other units. Starts and stops recorder when sound source starts and ends. Has "threshold" and "hold time" controls, and "override" switch.

 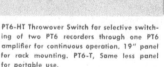  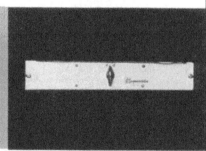

PT6-HT Throwover Switch for selective switching of two PT6 recorders through one PT6 amplifier for continuous operation. 19" panel for rack mounting. PT6-T, Same less panel for portable use.

PT6-H Rack Panel 19" x 8¾" for rack mounting PT6-AH or PT6-J. 71B139 Rack Mounting Adapter Plates, pair.

PT63-HT Throwover Switch for selective switching of two PT63-A recorders and one PT63 or PT7 amplifier for continuous operation. 19" panel for rack mounting. PT63-T same less panel for portable use.

See page 10 for specifications. Magnecordette models are shown in Catalog HF100.

THE NEW BINAURAL SYSTEM . . .

startling realism from tape

*Newest innovation in sound techniques does for
listening what stereography has done for seeing
in photography. By recording with two
microphones and playing back through independently
operated speakers or earphones sound acquires depth
and direction — a "presence" heretofore unknown.*

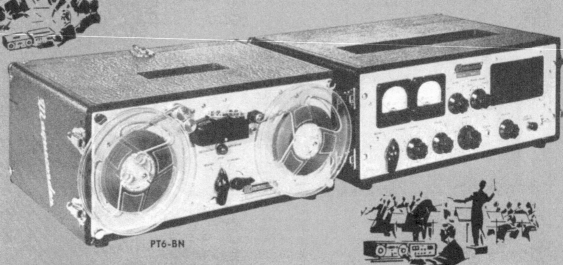

PT6-BN

Binaural recording, the recording method of the future, is available for the first time in a practical, portable and truly professional unit. Music recorded and played back binaurally produces an effect which defies description. Chorus and orchestra recordings are so realistic that conductors and performers alike are able for the first time to hear their performances as others hear them. Binaural recording thus not only permits unexcelled listening, but is an invaluable tool for the training of performers.

Individual voices in binaurally Magnecorded conferences stand out with the clarity and distinctiveness that increases transcribing efficiency. In industrial research, binaural noise analysis and vibration tests have provided engineers with a new tool revealing hitherto unavailable facts about product performance.

The new Binaural Magnecorder consists of two portable units, the PT6-BAH mechanical unit, and the PT6-BN amplifier. While normally supplied in portable cases, these units may readily be rack mounted in permanent installations.

The PT6-BAH mechanical unit is built to the well-known high standards of all Magnecord equipment. This unit uses two half track record/playback heads and a single erase head. Each half track head is fed from a section of the PT6-BN amplifier, to separately and simultaneously record two channels. The true spatial relationship of the original sound is thus recorded. This complete two channel record/playback mechanism also may be used in many industrial and research applications where two channel data or information recording is required.

The Binaural amplifier, PT6-BN, contains two independent record/playback channels, each with identical specifications. Two low impedance microphone inputs and balanced or unbalanced bridge inputs. Individual gain controls for each channel and a master control. Switch selects 7½ or 15 inch per second equalization. Calibration circuit permits interchannel balancing. Single speaker, fader-equipped, may be used on either channel. Two illuminated VU meters side by side for accurate level control. Two 10 watt power outputs tapped for 4 and 16 ohms. Each channel also has a 600 ohm zero level balanced or unbalanced line output.

PT6-BN amplifier may be used in portable case or directly rack mounted. PT6-BAH mechanical unit may be used in portable case or mounted in rack by means of an adaptor panel or plates.

magnecorder

the complete line of professional tape recorders

Great moments last through the years
when you record on tapes of Du Pont Mylar®

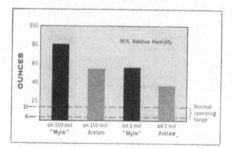

LASTING STRENGTH. In normal operation, recorders exert a force of 6 to 16 ounces. Graph shows tape of "Mylar" offers a 300% margin of safety against stretching or breaking.

Your favorite performances of classical music and jazz and treasured "family albums" sound vibrant and new through the years on trouble-free tapes of Du Pont "Mylar"® polyester film.

Here's why: Tapes of "Mylar" can not dry out or become brittle with age   offer an extra safety margin against stretching   are unaffected by changes in temperature and humidity. What's more, you get 50% or more longer playing time plus superior performance. So next time you buy, be sure to ask your dealer for your favorite brand of tape—make it two reels—made of "Mylar"

"Mylar" is a registered trademark for Du Pont's brand of polyester film. Du Pont manufactures "Mylar", not finished magnetic recording tape.

Better Things for Better Living ... through Chemistry

FOR THE BEST IN TAPE, LOOK FOR THE NAME "MYLAR" ON THE BOX

5

Polyester was cool in the 1950s.

*Reels! Tape erasers! Vibrators! These were some buzzwords
of the recording industry of the early 1950s.*

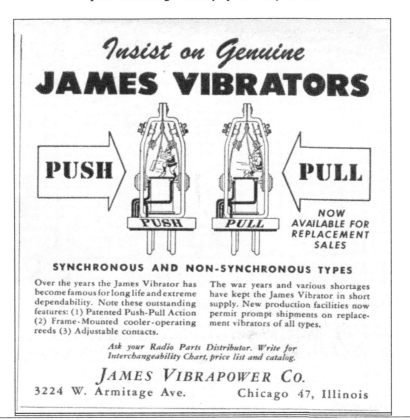

The stars come out for Revere!

Many of the World's leading artists
in the music and entertainment field use
and personally endorse the Revere Tape
Recorder. Their praise is *your* assurance
of recording satisfaction.

Star of Stars ...for Your Listening Pleasure!

Glenn Ford, too, chooses

Revere

"Balanced-Tone"

TAPE RECORDER

As a true perfectionist, Glenn Ford selects the tape recorder of his choice—a Revere "Balanced-Tone" Tape Recorder. Professionals invariably prefer the amazing "balanced-tone" a patented Revere exclusive—because they recognize that its inimitable high fidelity is comparable to costly studio equipment. Yet these lightweight, handsomely styled recorders combine rich tonal quality with operational ease to make them ideal for the home, as well. For the utmost in high fidelity recording and an unforgettable experience in listening pleasure, join the stars—make your choice a Revere "Balanced-Tone" Tape Recorder. See your Revere dealer today for a FREE demonstration!

Model T-700-D—(above) 3¾ and 7½ speeds. Simplified keyboard controls; automatic index counter for easy location of any portion of recorded reel; records up to 3 hours per 7" reel with new long-play tape. Complete with microphone, radio attachment cord, two reels (one with tape) and carrying case $212.50

Model TR-800-D—Same as above
with radio $265.00

Model T-1100 (right) 3¾ and 7½ speeds. Single knob control; records up to 3 hours per 7" reel with new long-play tape; dual acoustically matched speakers. Complete with 2 reels, tape and carrying case $159.50

Model TR-1200—Same as above with
radio $209.50

*Glenn Ford,
star of Metro-Goldwyn-Mayer's
"Interrupted Melody"*

REVERE CAMERA COMPANY
CHICAGO 16, ILLINOIS

Actor Glenn Ford poses with a Revere "Balanced-Tone" recorder in 1956. The advertisement touts the recorder as one preferred by professionals, mainly hi-fi enthusiasts.

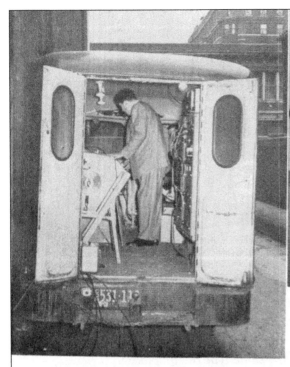

Left: the portable sound recording truck of Fine Sound, Inc. is loaded with equipment. Here it is parked in an alley behind Detroit's old Orchestra Hall ready to record the music from inside. Above: recording engineer Aaron Nathanson checks one of the Fairchilds inside the truck. The monitor speaker is above the recorder.

Top: On-location recording was only beginning when Fine Sound, the well-known New York studio, recorded a performance of Detroit's symphony orchestra in 1956. The operations truck was parked in an alley behind the music hall that day. Magnetic Film & Tape Recording magazine wrote a feature about the sound achievement. Bottom, a group confers before a live recording is recorded. At far left is Bert Berlant of Berlant recorder fame. Harvey Fisher, the radio and amp king, stands third from the left. With National Symphony and Jensen Manufacturing reps, they are hooking up two recorders, ten 50-watt Fisher amps, and ten Imperial speakers.

Build this ELECTRONIC MIXER

. . . with this unit you can mix two microphones and a phonograph.

In the early days of tape recording, you couldn't walk into a store and buy mixers and consoles and whatever else you needed to equip a studio and start making records. You had to build the equipment yourself or find someone else to do it. This period, the late 1940s through the '50s, is a fascinating one because there was so much custom-built equipment made each studio different. Today, studios are too much alike if they have the same type of equipment.

Narrow tape that can be edited without waste also saves storage space and postage on voice letters. Five reels in each stack. Demi-tape is on the right.

New Width Planned for Magnetic Tape

. . . "Demi-tape," only one-eighth inch wide may set second standard. Will play on all recorders. Makes editing easy.

Hi Fi and Tape Recording *magazine of the mid-1950s discussed every facet of recording tape.*
(Courtesy *Hi-Fi Tape Recording*)

In the spring of 1955, Czech actors listen to a playback of their weekly satirical program in Radio Free Europe's studios in Munich. In this picture, the audio engineer splices Scotch brand tape on what appears to be an Ampex 300 professional-model tape recorder.

"SCOTCH" BRAND JUGGLES ATOMS
to produce the finest long play magnetic tape!

Years ago "SCOTCH" Brand pioneered modern magnetic tape—and solved a knotty technical problem at the same time. The problem? How to produce recording tape with a uniform, magnetically-responsive oxide surface for finest recording results.

"SCOTCH" Brand does it by making its own oxide coatings. It's a difficult job and *only* "SCOTCH" Brand does it — splitting atoms to transform non-magnetic oxide into a *super*-magnetic coating sensitive enough to record even a whisper! But this extra work is worth the effort, as you'll hear yourself. *Today*—listen to a reel of new "SCOTCH" Brand

Extra Play Magnetic Tape 190. It offers you 50% more recording time on a standard-size reel, *plus* complete fidelity and purity of sound.

Electron photo microscope shows the difference!

At left, artist's conception of magnified view of old-fashioned oxide coating. At right, "SCOTCH" Brand lays on its own regular-shape, *super*-magnetic particles to give you a super-sensitive recording surface.

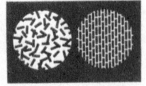

 Magnetic Tape 190
with 50% more recording time

 The term "SCOTCH" and the plaid design are registered trademarks for Magnetic Tape made in U.S.A. by MINNESOTA MINING AND MFG. CO., St. Paul 6, Minn. Export Sales Office: 99 Park Ave., New York 16, N.Y.   © 1955 3M Co.

In the fall of 1955, Scotch and Ampex again appeared in a tape ad. It featured electron microscopes and "super-magnetic particulars," fit for a sci-fi movie about UFOs.

Don't try this at home. It could be done only in the '50s.

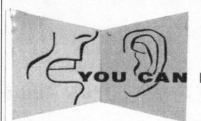

YOU CAN EDIT THE SOUND
as you record
WITH THIS VERSATILE
NEW *American Microphone*

Selective recording is easy with AMERICAN's new TRC microphone. You can hold the push button to talk, or "lock it on" for extended use. A handy clip-on stand is supplied for resting the microphone on conference tables... lavalier cord is also supplied.

With the sleek, modern TRC, you can take full advantage of your tape recorder's range .. at low cost. Choose from dynamic, ceramic, or crystal models. Wide frequency response (from 70 to 10,500 c.p.s. in the crystal model), omni-directional pickup, and faithful audio reproduction are yours for as little as $16.00 list price.

TRC *204 Series Microphones List Prices $16.00 to $24.30*

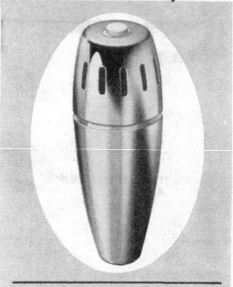

for professional quality public address and sound recording
AMERICAN's D22 Omni-directional Dynamic Microphone (with variable impedance)

This slender, graceful black-and-gold microphone sounds as good as it looks. Its smooth peak-free response (from 40 to 13,000 c.p.s.) means you virtually eliminate feedback problems and get wonderful performance. If you want quality, efficiency, and dependability—if you want a versatile microphone to use in hand or stand—if you want a microphone that's a stand-out in appearance—you want the D22.

D22 *List Price $99.50, shipped in Jewel-Box Case*

D33 *Broadcast model, with smooth flat response from 35 to 15,000 c.p.s. Jewel-Box Case. List Price $130.00*

Write for your free copy of the new AMERICAN MICROPHONE catalog, giving complete specifications on these and other fine AMERICAN microphones, handsets, cartridges, and tone-arms.

American Microphone MANUFACTURING COMPANY
a division of GC-Textron Inc.

West Coast Plant: Los Angeles 18, California
MAIN PLANT: 41½ SOUTH WYMAN STREET, ROCKFORD, ILLINOIS, U.S.A.
Export and Canada: Telesco International Corporation, 36 W. 40th St., New York, N.Y.

9

More mics from the 1950s—American-made.

In the mid-'50s, the "magnificent
Ferrograph" was hot. Heavy as a truck, too.

FEN-TONE MIKE

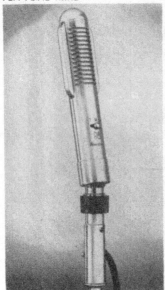

Fenton Company, 15 Moore Street, New York 4, N. Y., is marketing the Danish-made B&O-50, the third Fen-tone Blue Ribbon mike introduced this year. It is recommended for broadcasting, TV and movie studios, tape recording, and indoor public address use. This beautifully styled mike is 50 ohms impedance pressure gradient full bass and has a perfect figure 8 directional pattern, a three-way switch with "Close Talk," "Music," and "Off" positions, and a ball swivel mounting for easy tilting in any direction. Frequency range is 30—15,000 cps, plus or minus 2½ db; weight is less than 15 oz., size is 7-3/4" x 1-3/16"; and it is double screened against blast and entirely shock-proof. This mike is priced at $48.95, and additional information is available from the manufacturer.

STACK-A-RACK

Leslie Creations, P.O. Box 9516, Department 377, Philadelphia 49, Pa., has designed a handy storage rack. The Stack-A-Rack will accommodate recorded tapes, 45 RPM records, or reading matter, and it's top shelf will hold a radio, record player, planter, or other item. It features a unique "expansion" principle, and several racks may be stacked together; it's legs are rubber tipped; and it is available in black wrought iron at $6.95, or gleaming brass plate at $8.95, postpaid. For additional information, write to Leslie Creations.

(Continued on page 43)

Special trade-in allowances . . .
at all BERLANT-CONCERTONE Distributors

AKRON—Olson Radio, 75 E. Mills
ALBANY—Edwin E. Taylor Co., 465 Central Ave.
ALEXANDRIA, VA.—Certified Electronic
1330 Powhatan St.
ATLANTA—Baker Fidelity Corp.
1429 Peachtree St., N.E.
Gates Radio Co., 13 and Spring Sts.
BALTIMORE—High Fidelity House
5123 Roland Ave.
BATTLE CREEK—Electronic Supply Corp.
94 Hamblin Ave.
BERKELEY, CALIF.—Audio Shop
2497 Telegraph Ave.
BEVERLY HILLS—Minthorne Music Co.
230 North Beverly Drive
BIG SPRING, TEX.—High Fidelity House
503 Edwards Bldg.
BOSTON—Lafayette Radio, 110 Federal St.
The Listening Post, 161 Newbury St.
Radio Shack, 167 Washington
BROADVIEW, ILL.—Hi-Fi Unlimited
1303-05 Roosevelt Road
BROOKLYN—Benray Electronics Corp.
485 Coney Island Ave.
BUFFALO—Arrowlite Company, Inc., 326 Elm St.
Buffalo Audio Center, 153 Genesee
Frontier Electronics, 1505 Main St.
BURBANK—Collins Radio Co., 2700 West Olive
CAMBRIDGE—Hi-Fi Lab Electronic Supply
1077 Massachusetts Ave.
CEDAR RAPIDS—Collins Radio Co.
CHAMPAIGN, ILL.—New Sound
35 East Springfield Ave.
CHICAGO—Allied Radio, 100 N. Western Ave.
Electronic Expediters, 2909 West Devon Ave.
Musichron Corporation, 117 West Grand Ave.
Newark Electric Co., 223 West Madison St.
Voice & Vision, Inc., 53 East Walton
CLEVELAND—Olson Radio Warehouse
2020 Euclid Ave.
CONCORD, N. H.—Evans Radio
DALLAS—Town North Music Corp.
12 Inwood Shopping Village
DETROIT—Hi-Fi Studios, 8300 Kenkell
K.L.A. Laboratories, 7422 Woodward Ave.
Pecar Electronic Services, 10729 Morang
EAST ORANGE, N. J.—Custom Music Systems
426 Main St.
FARGO, N. D.—Wolter Electronic Co.
402 N. P. Ave.
GLENDALE—Glendale Electronics, 145 S. Brand
GRAND RAPIDS, MICH.—Radio Parts, Inc.
542-548 Division Ave., S.
HARTFORD, CONN.—Nathan Margolis Shop
28 High St.
HEMPSTEAD, LONG ISLAND—Island Radio Distributor, Inc., 412 Fulton Ave.
HOLLYWOOD—California Sound Products
7264 Melrose Ave.
Hollywood Electronics Supply, 7460 Melrose Ave.
Pacific Hi-Fi House, 1320 Cahuenga Blvd.
Recorders Distributors, 7115 Melrose Ave.
HOUSTON—Audio Center, Inc., 1633 Westheimer
Busacker Electronic Equip., 1216 W Clay
Gates Radio Co., 2700 Polk Ave.
Wrye Co., Ltd., 2045 Welch
INDIANAPOLIS—Graham Electronic Supply
102 South Pennsylvania St.
INGLEWOOD, CALIF.—Newark Electric Co.
4736 West Century Blvd.
JACKSON, TENN.—Carlton Wholesale Radio
312 S. Shannon
KALAMAZOO—Electronic Supply Corp.
906 East Michigan Ave.
KANSAS CITY, MO.—David Beatty Sound
1616 Westport Road
KNOXVILLE, TENN.—McClung Appliances
510 Georgia St., N.E.
LAFAYETTE, IND.—Lafayette Radio Supply, Inc.
Branch of Braham Electronics, 408 North St.
LANSING, MICH.—Offenhauser Co.
227 West Washtenaw St.
LAS VEGAS—Radio Sound Supply
25 E. California St.
LAWRENCE, KAN.—Snodgrass Electronics
733 Missouri St.
LOS ANGELES—Bushnell's Electronics
12026 Wilshire Blvd.
Crenshaw Hi-Fi Center, 3857½ Santa Rosalia Dr.
Gates Radio Co., 7501 Sunset Blvd.
Hannon Engineering Co., 5290 West Washington
Justin Kramer Associates, 3112 W Olympic Blvd.

Kierluff Sound Corp., 820 W Olympic Blvd.
L.A. Portable Recording Enterprises
521 N. La Cienega Blvd.
Midway Electronic Supply Co.
2817 Crenshaw Blvd.
MEMPHIS—Bluff City Dist. Co., 234 East St.
MIAMI—High Fidelity Associates
3888 Biscayne Blvd.
MILWAUKEE—Wack Sales Co., Inc.
3131 W North Ave.
MINNEAPOLIS—Paul A. Schmitt Music Co.
88 S. 10th St.
NASHVILLE—Electric Distributing Co.
1914 W End Ave.
NEWARK—Magnetic Recording, 528 Central Ave.
NEW BRUNSWICK, N. J.—The Jabberwock
104 Somerset St.
NEW ORLEANS—Electronic Parts Corp.
223-225 North Broad
NEW YORK CITY—Arrow Electronics
65 Cortlandt St.
Consolidated Sales, 768 Amsterdam Ave.
Davega Stores, (See Telephone Directory)
Federated Electronic Sales, Inc.
185 Washington St.
Gates Radio Co., 51 East 42nd St.
Goody Audio Center, 235 West 49 St.
Grand Central Radio, Inc., 124 East 44th St.
Hudson Radio & TV Corp., 48 West 48th St.
Leonard Radio, 69 Cortlandt St.
Milo Trading Co., 215 Fulton St.
Radio Wire Television, 100 Sixth St.
Recording Wire & Tape Co., 163 East 87th St.
Sonocraft Corporation, 115-117 West 45th St.
Sun Radio & Electronics Co., Inc., 650 Sixth Ave.
Terminal Radio, 85 Cortlandt St.
Julius Weikers & Co., 307 Audubon Ave.
NORFOLK, VA.—Electronic Engineering Co., Inc.
316 W Olney Road
PASADENA—High Fidelity House
534 South Fair Oaks
PATERSON, N. J.—Magnetic Recording
344 Main St.
PHILADELPHIA—Radio Electric Service Co. of Pa.,
Inc., 701 Arch St.
PITTSBURGH—Wolk's Hi Fi Center
308 Diamond St.
PORTLAND, ORE.—L. D. Heater Music Co.
1930 N. W Irving St.
PRINCETON, N. J.—Princeton Music Center
7 Palmer Square West
QUINCY, ILL.—Gates Radio Co.
RENO—Art Rempel Sound Services, 460 Wells Ave.
ROCHESTER—Jerry Fink Co., 644 Clinton Ave. S.
SALEM, ORE.—Cecil Farnes Co.
442 No. Church St.
SALT LAKE CITY—Poll & Austin, 1651 S. 11th E.
SAN DIEGO—Breier Sound Center
3781—5th Ave.
SAN FRANCISCO—C. R. Skinner Co.
239 Grant Ave.
Eber Electronics, 160 10th St.
San Francisco Radio and Supply Co.
1282 Market St.
SCHENECTADY—House of Harmony
1034 Eastern Ave.
SEATTLE—Electricraft, Inc., 622 Union
Seattle Radio Supply, 2117 Second Ave.
SPOKANE—20th Century Sales, Inc.
West 1021 First Ave.
ST. LOUIS—Commercial Electronics Service Co.
2609 Olive St.
Van Sickle Radio Co., 1113 Pine St.
SYRACUSE—Morris Distributing Co.
1153 W. Fayette St.
TUCKAHOE, N. Y.—Boynton Studios
10 Pennsylvania St.
WASHINGTON, D. C.—Electronic Wholesalers
2345 Sherman Ave., N.W.
Gates Radio Co., 13th and E Sts. N.W
Hi Fidelity Wholesalers
1327 Connecticut Ave., N.W
Laboratory of Electronic Engr., 413 L St. N.W.
WEBSTER GROVES, MO.—WBPA Sound Systems
132 West Big Bend
WILDWOOD, N. J.—The Music Center
239 East Oak Ave.
CANADA
Toronto—Custom Sound & Vision
390 Eglinton Ave., West
MEXICO
Ensenada, Baja California—DBA Custom Hi-Fi
Installation, P. O. 98, Riviera Pacific

Berlant Concertone ®

• *Audio Division of American Electronics, Inc.*

Berlant Concertone, a division of American Electronics, was one of the earlier tape recorder makers in the United States. Its machines were used by professionals as well as amateurs. In the mid-1950s, Hi Fi Tape Recording *magazine ran an advertisement that listed the company's distributors across the country. Perhaps one was located in your city. (Courtesy* Hi-Fi Tape Recording*)*

A shapely connector, 1948. The ad guys for Cannon and Malloy must have had fun in those days.

NEW SHURE "900MG"

CRYSTAL PHONOGRAPH PICKUP for

MICRO-GROOVE RECORDS

Provides Vast New Sales Fields For Dealers and Servicemen

The long-playing micro-groove records have opened a vast new sales field for Servicemen and Dealers. Hundreds of thousands of record enthusiasts are ready to buy the new records, but they must have a new pickup to play them. This is your big opportunity to "adapt" their present sets with the Shure "900MG." It is a tremendous market—an immediate, anxious, impatient market. Here are opportunities, sales, PROFITS! Think of the hundreds of phonograph users in your immediate area. You will render an outstanding service by using a Shure "900MG." It is unsurpassed for the most brilliant reproduction of music you have ever heard.

AVAILABLE AT SHURE DISTRIBUTORS NOW!

Model 900MG   Code: RUZUZ   List Price — $12.50

(Shure Patents Issued and Pending. Licensed under Patents of Brush Development Co.)

SHURE BROTHERS, INC.

Microphones and Acoustic Devices

255 W. HURON ST., CHICAGO 10, ILL. • CABLE ADDRESS: SHUREMICRO

20

Phonograph pickup, 1948. Tape was looming in the marketplace.

Russ Molloy of Bel Canto Records helped promote Scotch brand recording tape in the late 1950s.

PROFESSIONAL QUALITY
POPULAR PRICE!

Why do network news services rely on "SCOTCH" Magnetic Tape for recording on-the-spot news reports from all over the world? Dependability Matchless dependability inch after inch, reel after reel. This same professional quality is yours at no extra cost in famous "SCOTCH" Brand Tape for home recording

"SCOTCH" Brand alone offers you silicone lubrication—a built-in protection for your recorder head and precision oxide dispersion for controlled uniformity that gives you flawless response.

REG. U.S. PAT. OFF.

SCOTCH Magnetic Tapes
BRAND

"SCOTCH" IS A REGISTERED TRADEMARK OF 3M CO., ST. PAUL 6, MINN. EXPORT: 99 PARK AVE., NEW YORK 16, CANADA: LONDON, ONTARIO.

MINNESOTA MINING AND MANUFACTURING COMPANY
...WHERE RESEARCH IS THE KEY TO TOMORROW

This wasn't your mother's Scotch tape. It was a MMM miracle of sound in the '50s.

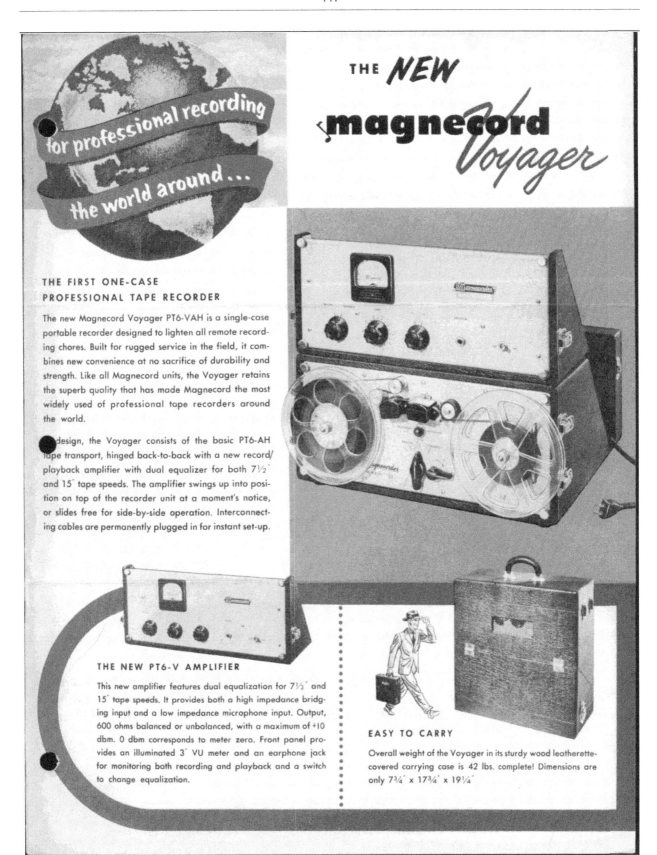

THE FIRST ONE-CASE PROFESSIONAL TAPE RECORDER

The new Magnecord Voyager PT6-VAH is a single-case portable recorder designed to lighten all remote recording chores. Built for rugged service in the field, it combines new convenience at no sacrifice of durability and strength. Like all Magnecord units, the Voyager retains the superb quality that has made Magnecord the most widely used of professional tape recorders around the world.

In design, the Voyager consists of the basic PT6-AH tape transport, hinged back-to-back with a new record/playback amplifier with dual equalizer for both 7½" and 15" tape speeds. The amplifier swings up into position on top of the recorder unit at a moment's notice, or slides free for side-by-side operation. Interconnecting cables are permanently plugged in for instant set-up.

THE NEW PT6-V AMPLIFIER

This new amplifier features dual equalization for 7½" and 15" tape speeds. It provides both a high impedance bridging input and a low impedance microphone input. Output, 600 ohms balanced or unbalanced, with a maximum of +10 dbm. 0 dbm corresponds to meter zero. Front panel provides an illuminated 3" VU meter and an earphone jack for monitoring both recording and playback and a switch to change equalization.

EASY TO CARRY

Overall weight of the Voyager in its sturdy wood leatherette-covered carrying case is 42 lbs. complete! Dimensions are only 7¾" x 17¾" x 19¼"

More Magnecord specs (see next page) from the 1950s. Good equipment, but at 42 pounds, who said it was easy to carry? Maybe it was for Georges "Superman" Reeves, but not for the 90-pound weaklings.

technical specifications

RECORDING SPEEDS: 15"/sec. and 7½"/sec. interchangeable, with no tools needed

REWIND SPEED: 1200 feet of tape (7" reel) 40 seconds

FREQUENCY RESPONSE: At 15"/sec. 50-15,000 cps, ± 2 db.

SIGNAL TO NOISE RATIO: Exceeds 55 db, with less than 3% harmonic distortion

INPUTS: One microphone input, 50 ohms impedance (may easily be changed to 200 ohm with soldering iron). One high impedance unbalanced input

OUTPUT: One 600-ohm output, balanced or unbalanced, 0 dbm corresponds to meter zero. Maximum output is +10 dbm.

MONITOR: One earphone monitor jack on the front panel, which is in the circuit in both Record and Playback

MOTORS: Hysteresis synchronous 117 v. 60-cycle AC drive motor. Shaded pole for rewind

FLUTTER: Max. 0.3%

POWER REQUIREMENTS: 110 v. 60-cycle AC only

DIMENSIONS: 7¾" x 17¾" x 19¼"

WEIGHT: 42 pounds

Magnecord INC.

PLANT AND OFFICES: 225 West Ohio Street, Chicago, Illinois

WORLD'S OLDEST AND LARGEST MANUFACTURER OF PROFESSIONAL MAGNETIC RECORDING EQUIPMENT

Among fans of tape recorders, Ampex, Scully, and Otari stand out. But what about Magnecord? The Chicago-based firm billed itself the "world's oldest and largest manufacturer of professional recording equipment." The company offered a wide variety of recording machines and products.

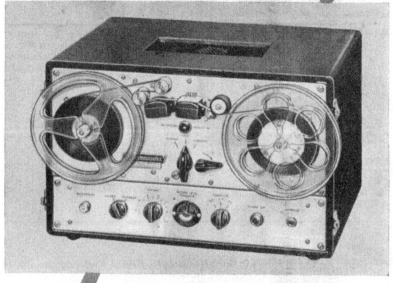
Magnecord promotes its new M-30 and M-33 in early 1954.

In use by 1949 were these Fairchild professional tape recorders. At that time tape recorders were made by Fairchild, Magnecord, Presto, RangerTone, RCA, Amplifier Corp. of America and Ampex Electric.

From Hi-Fi Tape Recording *magazine, mid-1950s.*

Left: this is an Ampex 200 tape recorder patterned after the German "Magnetophon" which used a special Minnesota Mining and Manufacturing Co. tape—No. 112—which was introduced in April of 1948. Subsequent Ampex recorders were modified to utilize 3M's red oxide tape No. 111. Tape speed of the Ampex 200, like the German "Magnetophon," was 30 inches per second. Right: tape recorder which was instrumental in switching the hundreds of radio stations over the country over to magnetic tape was the "Magnecorder" shown here, brought out in 1948. Magnecord started making professional wire recorders in 1946 but switched to tape.

Left: this 1949-50 professional tape recorder is a Stancil Hoffman unit in use today at radio station KULA in Honolulu. Right: professional tape recorders developed by RCA about 1950 are shown here. They were used, among other things, to record the Groucho Marx radio show.

From Hi-Fi Tape Recording Magazine, *mid-1950s.*

An early Bell tape recorder, c. early- to mid- 1950s.

Pete Bennett, left, of ABKKCO Industries, stands with record producer Phil Spector, left rear, and George Harrison as they listen to Harrison's All Things Must Pass *LP in late 1970.*

EVEN THE "ELECTRONIC EAR" OF STEREO HI-FI DIDN'T HEAR MISFIRING...

Recording a radio commercial outdoors, on what appears to be an Ampex 600. From 1956.

III.

Forgotten Recording Studios and Their Gear

". . .We may begin to wonder about the American tube manufacturers. Are they asleep? What's wrong with them if the European tubes are almost without exception better than our home product? Well, it's a long story. It involves mostly the relative lack of competition. . . ."

Jack Bayha
September 1957
Hi-Fi Tape Recording

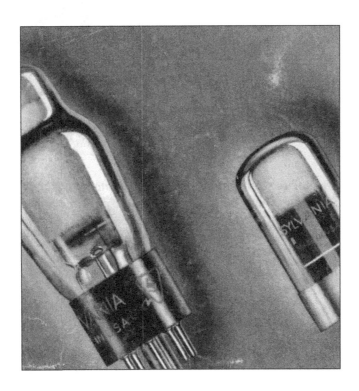

Bob Hope demonstrates the new Ampex 600, in 1954. The heavy but portable recorder was often used on location and by budget-conscious indie record producers in nightclubs.

THE NEW "600"

This new Ampex unit is typical of the simpler and less expensive versions of professional recorders available.

He ain't heavy, he's my Truvox, 1959.

.. fantastic!

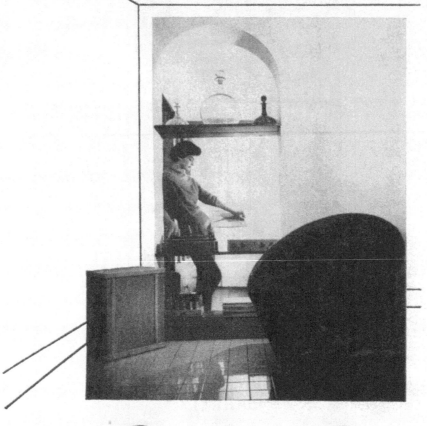

THE *Rebel*

KR - 5

20" CORNER FOLDED HORN

THE LITTLEST REBEL, The KR-5, approaches Klipschorn performance on light, middle bass. Heavy pipe organ bass is even more amazing with smooth, clean reproduction completely free from unmusical boom and distracting distortion. This latest Klipsch design by Cabinart, fifth in the CABINART-KLIPSCH REBEL series, is available in all fine woods, utility birch and, for portable hi-fi, strikingly smart leatherette.

Wall mount the Rebel 5, hang or set it in a corner. Place it on a table — a bench — a shelf — anywhere! Performance   absolutely unbelievable!

See your nearest Cabinart hi-fi dealer or write for catalogs.

Finished $48.00   Utility $33.00

 Cabinets by Cabinart   75 North 11th Street, Brooklyn 11, N. Y.

The Rebel, late 1954.

for high fidelity...today...and for years to come...

ONLY SOUNDCRAFT TAPES...

ONLY SOUNDCRAFT MICROPOLISHES TAPE!

Friction between recorder heads and non-polished tape surfaces is produced by tiny nodules...*microns in size*...which cause a loss of high frequency signals in recording, and even further loss in playback. Unless your tape surface is perfectly smooth when new...*you've lost high frequency* response before you start! Friction also causes dangerous head wear because recorder heads are forced to act as polishing surfaces! A truly smooth surface *must* be polished...and *no other tape*...ONLY SOUNDCRAFT TAPE is polished...MICROPOLISHED to guarantee high fidelity reproduction...to reduce head wear...*to save the quality of the sound!*

ONLY SOUNDCRAFT OXIDE FORMULATION IS PLASTICIZER-FREE!

Plasticizers, chemical agents used in other tapes to provide pliancy, eventually migrate into the atmosphere, leaving tape dry and brittle...*old before its time!* It is the oxide formulation on tape that carries the sound...and ONLY SOUNDCRAFT TAPES have the remarkable oxide formulation which eliminates antiquated plasticizers! You get *complete tape stability*...unequalled *protection for your recordings!* And when you buy SOUNDCRAFT TAPE on MYLAR* base you have double protection...*lifelong preservation of your recordings!*

* Dupont T.M.

PROFESSIONAL (Acetate)...professional applications—uniformity guaranteed. 7" reel—1200 feet.

RED DIAMOND (Acetate)...long, hard usage, economy. 7" reel—1200 feet.

ONLY SOUNDCRAFT OXIDE FORMULATION IS "UNI-LEVEL" COATED!

Variations in thickness of oxide coating cause distortion of low frequencies...a condition all the more dangerous because you can't see the variation. To insure faultless low frequency response through positive coating uniformity...*insist on* SOUNDCRAFT TAPES...the only tapes with oxide coating applied by the exclusive UNI-LEVEL process...*you can hear the difference!*

Because of these exclusive features, all SOUNDCRAFT TAPES offer complete uniformity...within a reel and from reel to reel...and can be freely interspliced without changes in volume!

PLUS 50 (Mylar)...long play, strength, long term storage. 7" reel—1800 feet.

PLUS 100 (Mylar)...extra-long play—ultimate in double-length tapes. 7" reel—2400 feet.

LIFETIME (Mylar)...utmost strength, professional fidelity, permanence, accurate timing—lifetime guarantee. 7" reel—1200 feet.

REEVES SOUNDCRAFT CORP.

10 E. 52nd Street, New York 22, N.Y. • West Coast: 342 N. La Brea, Los Angeles 36, California

FOR EVERY SOUND REASON...REFUSE LESSER QUALITY...BUY ONLY SOUNDCRAFT TAPES!

More Soundcraft tape advertising, 1957.

Speaking of Speakers...

DELCO RADIO CAREFULLY CONTROLS THE MANUFACTURING OF ITS SPEAKERS TO ASSURE HIGHEST POSSIBLE QUALITY

In the audio test booth, the speaker is checked for its ability to deliver good listening. In the background you can see a small section of the speaker production line.

High quality in the final product can be had only through rigid quality control. Take speakers, for example. Speaker baskets are formed in our stamping department. Special machines wind the voice coils. On the assembly line the cones are secured to the voice coils and then assembled with the basket. All along the line inspectors have been checking and rechecking. Then, the speaker is magnetized and goes into a specially designed sound booth for a final check.

This continuing quality control is one important reason why Delco Radio replacement parts assure customer satisfaction. Made by the world's largest manufacturer of auto radios, they are available from your UMS Delco Electronic Parts Distributor.

DISTRIBUTED BY
ELECTRONIC PARTS
DISTRIBUTORS
EVERYWHERE

DELCO RADIO
DIVISION OF GENERAL MOTORS CORPORATION, KOKOMO, INDIANA

A GENERAL MOTORS PRODUCT **GM** A UNITED MOTORS LINE

Delco promotes its speakers in 1954.

*Berry Gordy Jr., founder of Motown Records, operates the board
in his studio in Hitsville, the house he remodeled into his
label's headquarters and studio. Next page, the studio's main room.*

Motown Records' Studio A, where many of the label's hit were recorded. On the right side, Studio A's control room is visible. Next Page, the control room at Hitsville.

Motown's original recording control room, in the Hitsville house in Detroit, looked about the same in 2011 as it did in the early 1960s, when Berry Gordy Jr. was cutting hits that appealed to teenagers of all races. His sound was a slick version of R&B. In this studio display, rack-mounted recorders are conveniently located right behind what appeaers to be a custom-made board.

(Photo by Randy McNutt)

Pop vocalist Dusty Springfield in the control room of an English studio, with engineer, left, c. 1963.

*Can you hear it? Searching for natural sounds
with a parabolic reflector and recording them
with a portable Ampex, c. 1956.*

CROSSTALK

Hi Fi Tape Recording
July 1958

It is estimated that 80 percent of the recorders to be built next year will have the stereo playback feature incorporated in them. We think the industry's best bet is to bring out stereo recorders and thus keep one up in the one-upmanship game between discs and tape.

A Four-Channel Mixer

Radio and Television News
November 1954

Every recording studio except the very smallest has, on occasion, a need for audio mixing facilities. Unfortunately, most of the inexpensive mixing equipment that is commercially available is, at best, of amateur quality while professional-type equipment is usually priced in direction proportion to its quality.

"This program was taped recorded"? Radio Listeners heard this line a lot in the early 1950s.

Country singer Jim Reeves makes a point to audio engineer Bill Porter as producer
and RCA's Nashville A&R chief Chet Atkins looks on. Photo, from the 1960s, was taken at either RCA's
Studio B or A. Note the smaller console and speakers mounted on the wall.

The special console at Suma Recording, Painesville, Ohio, 2000. (Randy McNutt)

*Cincinnati country-rockabilly singer Rusty York opened Jewel
Recording in his garage in 1961. Later, he moved into a larger space.*

Radio personality Gary Burbank at the board at an unidentified radio station, most likely in Louisville, Kentucky, in the late 1970s or early 1980s. The cowboy standing nearby looks a lot like Roy Rogers. Note the turntable to Gary's left.
(Photo courtesy Mike Martini.)

This new amplifier, made in England, is advertised in the United States in the mid-1950s.

From 1957: Boom, Boom Boom.

From 1957: Inventor Paul Klipsch endorses Irish Shamrock tape.

Electro-Voice advertises to the hi-fi and professional scene in 1957.

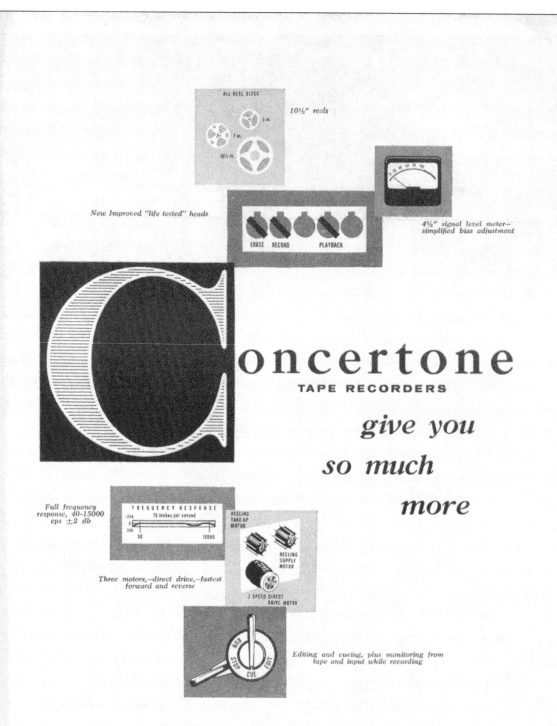

ALL REEL SIZES

10½" reels

New Improved "life tested" heads

ERASE RECORD PLAYBACK

4½" signal level meter—
simplified bias adjustment

oncertone
TAPE RECORDERS

give you

so much

more

Full frequency
response, 40-15000
cps ±2 db

FREQUENCY RESPONSE
15 inches per second

REELING
TAKE-UP
MOTOR

REELING
SUPPLY
MOTOR

2 SPEED DIRECT
DRIVE MOTOR

Three motors,—direct drive,—fastest
forward and reverse

Editing and cueing, plus monitoring from
tape and input while recording

AMERICAN ELECTRONICS, INC., one of the world's largest manufacturers of tape recorders, employs the skill and experience of hundreds of High Fidelity engineers and technicians in the development and manufacture of Concertone tape recorders. That's why independent surveys consistently show that Concertone is the first choice of audiophiles and audio pioneers.

The experience, production facilities, financial backing and engineering "know how" behind every Concertone assure you of lasting quality, satisfaction and dependability.

TAKE TIME TO PAY When you purchase your Concertone Custom Recorder you can pay as little as $49.50 down and $7.50 per week on the New Concertone Time Payment Plan. Ask your dealer for full particulars. For further information, write for Bulletin 4 F.

 AMERICAN ELECTRONICS, INC. *Audio Division*
655 W. Washington Blvd. • Los Angeles 15, California

Concertone gets aggressive with its advertising, 1957.

An unidentified engineer at the board, 1958. Location unknown.

The Scully at Counterpart

Randy McNutt (left) and production partner Wayne Perry
at the Electrodyne console in the Counterpart Studios, 1971.

For twenty years, a Cincinnati recording studio cut hits and provided work for dozens of studio musicians and songwriters. It wasn't the legendary King Recording Studio or the historic E.T. Herzog Recording. It was Counterpart Creative Studios, based in suburban Cheviot, Ohio, a small city that lies just west of Cincinnati in Hamilton County. Counterpart was not one of Cincinnati's early studios. It didn't open until 1971, but that was just in time to host some fine rock and soul bands and independent producers. In retrospect, Counterpart was an example of what the new American recording studio meant to music. It was a microcosm of the national studio business.

Fortunately, I was able to be a small part of Shad O'Shea's dream. I produced records there on a sixteen-track Scully recorder that I loved, and would come to love even more, as the years wore on.

Before O'Shea opened Counterpart Creative, local music people usually cut records at Jewel Recording in the nearby city of Mt. Healthy, Ohio, and at the famous King Recording Studios in Cincinnati's old Evanston neighborhood. King closed in 1971, when O'Shea's dreams of a recording studio began.

O'Shea founded Counterpart Creative for two simple reasons: He needed a business to support him, and he was tired of driving to Louisville to record rock bands for his Cincinnati-based Counterpart Records. The former WCPO Radio disc jockey already had hit regionally—from Lexington, Kentucky, to Indianapolis and up to Columbus—with his Counterpart label from 1963 to 1970. He also operated a BMI song-publishing firm with the name Counterpart Music. He worked with garage bands such as the Mark V, the New Lime, and the US Too Group. A lot of people in Cincinnati assumed that Counterpart Records was a national label because it placed so many hits in regional cities' top-10 lists during the golden age of the garage band.

By the late 1960s, O'Shea was one of Ohio's busiest independent producers. He recorded his own novelty songs as well as artists from the major musical genres. Many of his productions ended up being released on Counterpart first, and later on other hot independents or the major labels.

"In those days," O'Shea explained, "you could find a rock band and cut a record for $500 and put out a single that would get a lot of play from radio stations in your region. There were a lot of regional hits in the days before radio stopped playing small labels. This is how Counterpart Studios was born. It all happened after I did so many records in the 1960s."

In the early 1970s, Counterpart Creative welcomed performers who would later go on to success with the larger labels and song publishers. They cut the studio's initial tracks on O'Shea's sixteen-track Scully. He produced Bobby Borchers' commercial and haunting country single "Harlan," initially released on Counterpart Records. When the recording received modest but enthusiastic response, the singer relocated to Nashville and wrote hits by Johnny Paycheck and other country stars. The "Harlan" session featured Cincinnati's top studio players. O'Shea also cut a big-sound ballad called "A Song for Peace," by Mike Reid, a singer-pianist and a football player who had just quit the Cincinnati Bengals to launch a career in music. His original ballad, with strings and horns, was appropriate in the Vietnam War days. O'Shea sold the master to Laurie Records of New York. Although it wasn't a big hit, it did launch Reid's songwriting career in Nashville.

Counterpart also started a production and writing career for singer Wayne Perry, a young songwriter from Hamilton, Ohio, who recorded four singles at the studio for release on Counterpart Records. Perry later became a hit songwriter in

Nashville, writing for the Back Street Boys, Lorrie Morgan, and Joe Diffie. Perry's first single, "Mr. Bus Driver," was a driving soul-rocker that was leased to Avco-Embassy Records in New York. It was written by the talented Wayne Carson Thompson. When the company failed to release it, O'Shea agreed to put it out on Counterpart. (It had been recorded at the Jewel Studio.)

Gene Lawson, who engineered Perry's recording at Jewel, joined O'Shea's new studio as engineer a short time later, and oversaw the remainder of Perry's sessions at Counterpart. Meanwhile, O'Shea recorded a number of his own novelty singles for his label. Soon after the studio opened, he became one of the most prolific novelty producers in the nation. He wrote and recorded satirical and crazy songs such as "Back to Nature" by Hy Bush and the Wild Cranberries. In 1975, he purchased the rights to the name Fraternity Records, a label started by Harry Carlson in Cincinnati in 1954. With hits (all recorded at King) such as "Memphis" by Lonnie Mack and "Then You Can Tell Me Goodbye" by the Casinos, the Fraternity label became a leading Midwest independent through 1967. After purchasing the company, which O'Shea relocated from the Sheraton Gibson Hotel in downtown Cincinnati to Counterpart Creative in Cheviot, O'Shea started releasing most of his own records on Fraternity. The Counterpart label slowly faded into history. It is now owned by a New York company. Although O'Shea's novelties weren't big hits, they were wacky enough to receive airplay on hundreds of stations nationally. Recorded at Counterpart Creative were "Colorado Call," a spoof of the citizens band radio craze by Shad O'Shea and the 18-Wheelers (Fraternity and Private Stock), and "McLove Story," a salute to McDonald's ubiquity by Shad O'Shea and the Hamburger Helpers (Fraternity and SSS International).

In the late 1970s, O'Shea bought a new twenty-four track Scully recorder and sold his old sixteen-tracker. In the early 1980s, Counterpart Creative recorded single hits and albums by R&B groups such as Midnight Star on Solar Records, and the group Sun on Capitol. Midnight Star, a band formed in 1976 in Louisville, featured Reggie Calloway, who would later become a producer and operate the old QCA Studios in Cincinnati. Star's R&B hit "No Parking (On the Dance Floor)" came from an album that was recorded at Counterpart Creative and Fifth Floor Recording in Cincinnati. In addition, R&B singers Roger and Tony Troutman, area R&B singers, also recorded at Counterpart, as did the band Cannon, with some former members of the Casinos.

As I look back on Counterpart's history, I can see how it mirrored the history of every recording studio in every town. It meant more than a collection of wires, mics, baffles, and recorders. It meant personal experiences and music that made us happy. This was so at Counterpart. But the sixteen-track Scully's story did not end with the arrival of its more sophisticated relative. In 1988, I finished writing a book called *We Wanna Boogie*, about America's rockabilly performers of the 1950s. One of the guys I had profiled was Bill Watkins, a Cincinnati country and rockabilly singer and the owner of a basement studio named Tip Toe Recording. Bill was the engineer. After the book was published in 1989, Bill called and asked if I would like to see Tip Toe and maybe record there. I entered the basement and spotted his Scully. "I used to record on a Scully just like this one over at Counterpart," I said, gushing a bit. "I loved that machine. I have no idea what ever happened to it." He looked at me and smiled. "Well, I do. You're looking at it." The Scully cranked on as we cut two rockabilly albums, three singles, and a nationally charted record. In time, it started breaking down, but thanks to some tinkering it would come back to life. Bill always found a sound man who could take the Scully out of the intensive care unit. Finally, one day it stopped. That was the end. No longer could Bill find a repair man or the much-needed parts. He drove his pickup truck to New York to buy another Scully, just like his old one. Unfortunately, things did not work out. He had to sell both of them and buy a more modern eight-track machine, a semi-pro model. It sounded good, but nothing like the powerful Scully. That machine did some heavy lifting.

But back to the late 1980s. As the decade ended, studio competition became tougher and business slowed for O'Shea. He sold the studio's contents in 1991, and moved his companies—Fraternity Records, song publishing firms, and his new Positive Feedback Communications book publishing—into an office in a Cheviot office building. He continued to operate there as an independent producer, label owner, and author, writing how-to books about the music industry. In 2007, he semi-retired and sold the Fraternity name and his publishing companies.

He also sold the remaining pieces of the studio that he had loved so much: a sign that had once hung in the lobby, and record awards that had covered the walls of his office. Nearly everything in the place went in a sale. He gave me a framed color photograph of the interior of the studio. I cherish it to this day.

"The record business as I knew it is dead," O'Shea told me in June 2007. "Judging by today's standards, it's difficult to believe that the business was once such an exciting field to work in. The phone used to ring off the hook every day with disc jockeys, distributors, and studio people calling. It was a great thing to be a part of, but it has changed. The big studios aren't needed so much anymore with all the good home recording equipment. Now it's all computers and the Internet and so forth. But at least I lived during the heyday of the music business. I wouldn't trade the experience for anything."

Nor would I. Memories of that old Scully still make me smile.

Fast Facts

Name: Counterpart Creative Studios.

Address: 3744 Applegate Avenue, Cheviot, Ohio

Owner-manager: Shad O'Shea.

Location: In residential area, in a remodeled 1930s house.

Studio Rooms: One.

Initial Equipment: Sixteen-track Scully tape recorder (later upgraded to a 24-track recorder); Electrodyne console.

Engineers: Gene Lawson, Wes Owen, Dale Smith, and others.

Quirks: Inside the lobby was a long wall covered with about 125 singles that O'Shea had produced or with which he had been associated. All were on national labels, including Mercury, Era, Capitol, RCA, and Monument. As soon as a client entered the building, he saw the wall. O'Shea kept it that way until he remodeled the studio in the 1980s.

Some Notable Clients: Aerosmith, Livingston Taylor, Rob Hegel, The Zap Band, Bootsy Collins, Leonard Bernstein, Midnight Star, Sun, Mike Reid, the Ohio Players, Roger Troutman, Lamb, Bobby Borchers, and Wayne Perry.

House Band: None. But over two decades prominent Cincinnati musicians in pop, country, jazz, and rock recorded at Counterpart, including pianist Dumpy Rice, drummer Gene Lawson, and arranger Gordon Brisker.

Associated Enterprises: Under one roof were Counterpart Records, Applegate Recording Society, Bunk House Records, Counterpart Music (BMI), Hurdy Gurdy Music (ASCAP), Fraternity Records, PFC, and other music-related businesses operated by O'Shea.

Most Discussed Single that Didn't Hit: "Space Funk" by the funk group Manzel, released on Fraternity in 1977. "It could be the most-sampled record in the world," O'Shea said.

First Take: Counterpart was only the second studio I had ever recorded in. Jewel Recording was the first. So my initial comparisons were inevitable. Jewel was terrific for a deep sound, the kind you'd want on an old R&B record or for Southern gospel. It helped "Mr. Bus Driver" become a real driving track. I was surprised to hear a brighter sound at Counterpart, which made the studio good for pop and rock, especially when acoustic guitars were used. Counterpart had a clear sound--very crisp. I enjoyed recording several singles there, and hearing many productions by Shad and other producers right there in the control room.

Where, Oh Where, Has Scully Gone?: O'Shea's first recorder, a 16-track Scully, was installed in late 1970 or early 1971. He used it for a few years, until he purchased a 24-tracker. I'm not certain where the first Scully went next, but I do know that it landed in the basement studio of rockabilly and country singer Bill Watkins in suburban Cincinnati about 1977. Bill bought it from somebody who lived in the area. At his Tip-Toe Recording Studios, Bill worked the old Scully hard for five to eight years, and then slowed down his pace of recording. By the time I was reunited with the Scully, the year was 1989. I soon learned that the machine was the same one on which I had cut four Wayne Perry rock singles and a country one by Ron Sweet at Counterpart Studios in the 1970s. Bill and I got busy recording rockabilly singles and albums at his studio after I wrote about him in my book *We Wanna Boogie: An Illustrated History of the American Rockabilly Movement* ($25; Amazon.com). We cut Bill's singles "Red Cadillac" and "Cowboy" at Tip-Toe, and then albums for the Rockhouse and Gee-Dee labels in Europe. Sadly, the Scully started breaking down not long after that time, and Bill couldn't find anybody to repair it anymore. He finally sold it to a guy in rural New York about 2004. From then on, Bill longed for the days of the Scully and its wonderful depth of sound.

In this 1973 photo, the author stands next to a sixteen-track Scully recorder in the control room at Counterpart Creative Recording in Cincinnati. At the board are studio owner Shad O'Shea, right, and an unidentified engineer. McNutt recorded six singles on Counterpart's machine. Then O'Shea sold it to Cincinnati rockabilly singer and audio engineer Bill Watkins, who installed it in his Tip Toe Recording Studio. Watkins used the recorder for nearly fifteen years. On it McNutt produced several singles and two albums for Watkins, including two nationally charted singles.

A Not-So-Groovy Situation

As magnetic audio tape and wire gained in popularity, makers of transcription equipment scrambled to stay relevant. Though they would remain in the audio business for years, their heyday would soon end. In this 1949 ad, Charles Michelson of New York announces the elimination of its playback department. This AC Porto Playback machine—used to play transcription discs in radio and TV stations and even in some recording studios—is being offered for $75—a good deal at the time. At twenty-six pounds, it is a heavy little thing, but it plays the regular size sixteen-inch transcriptions discs in the field or in the studio.

This stereo recorder from 1958 was designed to compete with the Ampex 600 series of recorders. Like the Ampex, the Roberts was relatively heavy at 28 pounds. Though lacking the faster speeds, this portable could be used professionally in the field by radio stations and ad agencies.

Early Home Recording Studios, 1955

John Morris of Australia records in his bedroom, 1955.

Below, an unidentified woman records with various instruments.

1n 1949, custom-built equipment was the primary source of consoles.

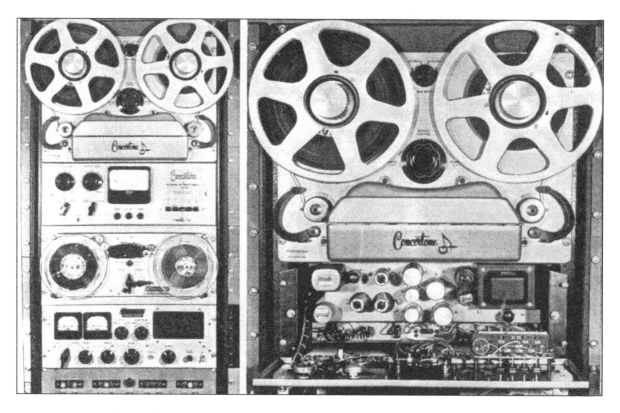

Find parts for this 1950 Concertone today, and you'll be an audio magician.

Berlant was there at the beginning, c. 1949

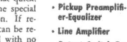

Amplifier Corporation of America and Fairfield Recording Equipment Company were ready by 1949.

By the mid-1950s, Audiotape was servicing both the pro and amateur tape-recording markets.

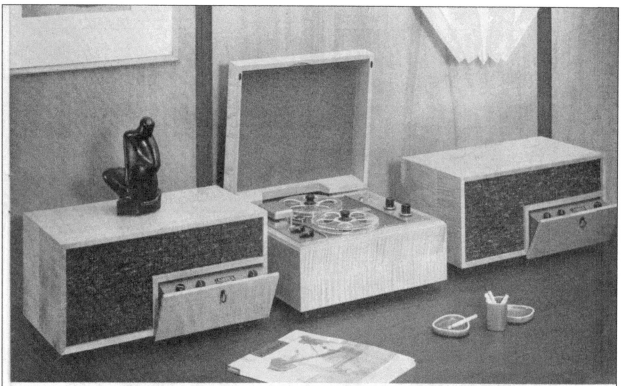

The Ampex 612-I Stereophonic Tape Phonograph and 620-f Amplifier-Speakers

the last word in living room listening...

AMPEX STEREOPHONIC SOUND

Once you've heard the Ampex 612 stereophonic tape phonograph system, you'll never be satisfied with less. It's the latest and the finest in listening pleasure, makes previous high fidelity seem old fashioned. The startling realism and magnificent quality of the 612 system brings a new panorama of sound into your living room — new heights in listening enjoyment that only a superb tape machine can achieve.

Not only does the 612 system capture all the depth and clarity of stereophonic sound, but its small size is really unique. Even the most critical audiophile is astonished that such big, clean

sound can come from such compact equipment. Complete with tape phonograph and two amplifier-speakers, it covers only four square feet of wall space for convenient placement in any living room.

With true Ampex quality, the Model 612 plays full-track, half-track or two track stereophonic tapes. Both the tape phonograph and the amplifier-speakers are available in handsome hardwood cabinets with either blonde or brunette finish. See and hear them today. Special stereophonic demonstrations are being featured this month at your Ampex Dealer's. *Ask about the Ampex Time Pay Plan.*

AMPEX
CORPORATION

Dealers in principal cities (see your local Telephone Directory under "Recording Equipment")
Canadian Distribution by Ampex American, 70 Grenville, Toronto, Ontario.
SIGNATURE OF PERFECTION IN SOUND
934 Charter Street, Redwood City, California.

Ampex invaded the home market in the late 1950s.

Christmas, 1958: Ampex goes after the home hi-fi market and semi-pro recordists.

NO MORE "UNFINISHED" SYMPHONIES!

WITH THE NEW SOUNDCRAFT "PLUS-50" MAGNETIC RECORDING TAPE! 50% EXTRA PLAYING TIME! NO COMPROMISE IN STRENGTH OR QUALITY!

HERE at last is the perfected "long-playing" magnetic tape. Backed with DuPont "Mylar" Polyester Film a third thinner than standard acetate backing—it is actually stronger than standard tapes.

A normal 5", 600' reel now holds 900'—a 7", 1200' reel holds 1800'. And yet cost-per-foot remains almost exactly the same!

Symphonies up to 48 minutes long can now be recorded or played at a full 7½" per second on a single 7" reel—without interruption. Forty-eight minutes against only 32 on standard tapes!

Soundcraft's fully perfected magnetic oxide is used—in *full, standard depth*—for utmost high fidelity. There's no change in output level or bias characteristics!

"Plus-50" is Micro-Polished® for perfect high-frequency response right from the start. It's Pre-Coated with adhesive to prevent oxide chipping, peeling. It's lubricated on both sides, eliminating squeals. It can be interspliced with any quality tapes. Output variation is an inaudible $\pm\,\frac{1}{4}$ db. within a reel, $\pm\,\frac{1}{2}$ db. reel-to-reel.

More than 200 million feet of this identical tape have already been supplied to the U. S. Government.

See for yourself why there's no finer tape at any price than Soundcraft "Plus-50" Tape. Get some at your dealer's today!

For more information, write Dept. U11.

FOR EVERY SOUND REASON

REEVES

SOUNDCRAFT

CORP.

10 E. 52nd St., N. Y. 22, N. Y.

By 1956, the Soundcraft company was advertising extensively in recording magazines.

TRU-SONIC THREE-WAY

Another new sight in sound from Stephens Tru-Sonic. Designed by Charles Eames and the Stephens Tru-Sonic engineering staff, this superb Three-Way speaker system was created for the most discriminating listener. The exclusive retractable horn provides tru-room dispersion and enables you to tune your system in proper balance to room acoustics. The full range— 20 to 20,000 cycles per second—and natural balance of the audio spectrum is obtained by this combination of a 103LX 15" low frequency woofer, a ten-cell retractable tru-exponential mid-range horn with a high frequency driver, a 214 Super Tweeter, and two crossover networks. Mounted on rigid aluminum legs, this revolutionary folded horn enclosure comes with a durable white micarta front and a choice of rare pal dao, teak, walnut or natural birch woods. Listen   you'll always hear more from

STEPHENS **TRU-SONIC** INC.   8538 Warner Drive, Culver City, California

Cable Address: "MORHANEX" • Export Address: 458 Broadway, New York 13, N.Y

By 1957, another speaker company, Tru-sonic, sought to fill the market for hi-fi fans and professionals.

In 1955, the Telectro model, made by the Telectronic Corporation of New York, was a lesser-known player in the pro tape recorder game.

3 MOTORS

3 HEADS

FAST FORWARD

the *new* SR-27
tape recorder

built to professional standards for high fidelity home use

FAST REWIND

10 WATT OUTPUT

LINE INPUT

LINE OUTPUT

NARTB SPECS

Here at last is a tape recorder that fits the gap between the expensive professional model and the small home recorder with its severely limited range. This Presto unit is the answer to a long-felt need for a portable tape recorder of professional quality at a price an amateur can afford.

The SR-27 consists of the new R-27 tape transport mechanism and the Presto A-920B amplifier. The R-27 embodies many design features of Presto's best professional models. It utilizes three individual magnetic heads to record, erase, and play back tape on 7-inch or on the new 8-inch reels with the NARTB hub.

Three separate motors are employed for smooth tape transport and fast-speed rewind. The capstan is driven by a hysteresis motor to insure timing accuracy. New, specially designed brakes are self-adjusting and self-aligning. A single control lever sets the mechanism for record, playback, or fast-speed operation, and the desired speed of 7½ or 15 inches per second is selected by moving the speed shift knob up or down.

The A-920B amplifier, furnished in a separate carrying case, contains microphone and playback pre-amplifiers, a power supply, and two speakers for playback at normal room level.

The SR-27 is the ideal unit for field use. It is heavy enough to stand plenty of rough treatment and will produce quality recording conforming to NARTB specifications. Broadcast stations and recording studios will find the SR-27 an ideal combination in which performance, size, and cost have been perfectly balanced.

A F-10/13/55

Presto! Another well-made machine arrives in 1955, and the maker is not a newcomer to the field.

R-27 MECHANISM

TAPE SPEEDS: 7½ and 15 ips, fast forward and rewind.

REEL SIZE: 8 inch, max.

NUMBER OF HEADS: Three

NUMBER OF MOTORS: Three (including hysteresis capstan motor).

BIAS/ERASE FREQUENCY: 85 kc.

OSCILLATOR TUBE: 6Y6G

POWER REQUIREMENT: 115 volts, 60 cycle, 210 watts. 50 cycle available at additional cost.

SIZE: 16" x 13" x 10" in carrying case.

WEIGHT: 39 lbs. in carrying case.

A-920B AMPLIFIER

MICROPHONE INPUT: 50 or 250 ohms.

ADDITIONAL INPUT: High level microphone or radio tuner.

OUTPUT: 10 watts at 15 ohms, zero db. line level at 500 ohms.

MONITOR OUTPUT: For high impedance phones to monitor incoming signal or tape output.

SELECTOR SWITCH POSITIONS: Record, playback, line feed, and public address system.

VOLUME INDICATOR: Illuminated, calibrated VU meter to monitor record level, bias, and line output level.

AMPLIFIER TUBES: Two 6J7, three 6SL7GT, two 6V6GT, one 5Y3GT.

SPEAKERS: Two 5-inch permanent magnet type.

POWER REQUIREMENT: 115 volts, 50 or 60 cycle, 110 watts.

SIZE: 20" x 9" x 8" in carrying case.

WEIGHT: 38 lbs. in carrying case.

PERFORMANCE DATA

FREQUENCY RESPONSE: Uniform from 50 to 15,000 cps at 15 in. per sec; uniform from 50 to 10,000 cps at 7½ in. per sec.

SIGNAL TO NOISE RATIO: Better than 50 db.

FLUTTER: Not more than 0.15% RMS at 15 in. per sec; 0.25% RMS at 7½ in. per sec.

TIMING ACCURACY: 3/10 to 1/2 of 1%.

RECORDING CHARACTERISTIC: NARTB specifications.

PRICE: SR-27 COMPLETE $588.00

PRESTO RECORDING CORPORATION
P O. BOX 500, PARAMUS, NEW JERSEY

World's Largest Manufacturer of Instantaneous Sound Recording Equipment and Discs

EXPORT DIVISION: 25 WARREN STREET, NEW YORK 7, N. Y

Canadian Distributor: Instantaneous Recording Service
42 Lombard Street, Toronto, Ont., Canada

SR-27-10M/9-55
PRINTED IN U. S. A.

The second page of the recorder's spec sheet shows its capability of running at fifteen inches per second.

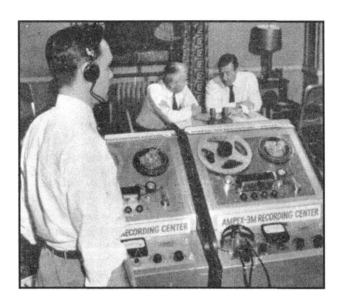

Experimenting with Ampex recorders and 3M tape, 1956.

Take note: In 1954, veterans were just as impressed with tape as the young ones.

Why only "Scotch" Magnetic Tape was qualified to record the

World's longest organ recital

In a monumental three-year project, Westminster Records has begun recording the complete organ works of Bach on the Varfrukyrka organ at Skanninge, Sweden.

Seven discs, released last summer, have already won plaudits both for the dedicated performance of organist Carl Weinrich and for the quality of their recorded sound. An auspicious beginning for a series which will eventually contain 22 records and require two more years to complete!

Discs, of course, are made from magnetic tape masters. Westminster found only *one* magnetic tape sensitive enough to capture the subtle overtones and baroque beauty of the Varfrukyrka organ—"Scotch" Magnetic Tape. In fact, "Scotch" Brand has been used by Westminster to make all master recordings for their distinguished "Lab" series. And no wonder. "Scotch" Brand offers superior frequency response . . . reel-to-reel uniformity and complete dependability.

Hear recorded sound as you've never heard it before—on "Scotch" Brand Magnetic Tape.

The term "Scotch" and the plaid design are registered trademarks for Magnetic Tape made in U.S.A. by MINNESOTA MINING AND MANUFACTURING CO., St. Paul 6, Minn. Export Sales Office; 99 Park Ave., New York 16, N.Y © 3M CO., 1956

ORGANIST CARL WEINRICH (right) and Westminster Musical Director Kurt List study the Varfrukyrka organ at Skanninge, Sweden.

Scotch and 3M were advertising again in 1955.

MAGNETIC FILM &

TAPE RECORDING

World's Leading
Recording Magazine

EXCLUSIVE!

TAPE COVERS
THE
CONVENTIONS

•

SHOW OFF
YOUR TAPES

RECORDING
BRASS
INSTRUMENTS

TAPE ON
THE NORTH
ATLANTIC

NEW PRODUCT
REPORT:

This magazine cover featured boxing Democrats and Republicans during their 1956 conventions. Tape recorders were used to record events for both parties. The magazine was devoted recording.

Rise Stevens listens to playback of magnetic tape on which voice, is recorded and then pressed into a disk. Single notes can be added or deleted by splicing.

From the Baltimore Sun, *July 25, 1954.*

Shure advertises its new microphones, mid-1950s.

NEW PRODUCT REPORT

AMERICAN RECORDER MICROPHONES

. . . ceramic and crystal models–light weight, small, 100-7000 cps range.

STAFF **OK** TESTED

Product: American Microphones Models B-203 and X-203

Manufacturer: American Microphone Co., 370 S. Fair Oaks, Pasadena, Calif.

Price: $8.35 list with RCA phono plug, $9.40 with miniature phone plug. $7.25 and $8.00 without plugs.

THESE two new microphones are encased in plastic (red, black, gray or beige) with a simulated gold grille. They are designed for durability, are of light weight and our tests showed that they also had good quality. Their size is small, measuring only 3¼" x 2⅛" x 1", and they have an unobtrusive and pleasing appearance.

Either mike weighs but two ounces and they may be hand held, placed on a flat surface or taped to the wall or fixtures.

The microphones are available in various colors. A five foot shielded cable is attached to each mike. Either RCA-type phono plugs or miniature phone plugs are supplied with the mikes at slight additional cost.

The output of both mikes is high impedance with a —55 db level for the X-203 crystal type and —62 db for the B-203 ceramic. These outputs make the mikes suitable for most non-professional recorders.

The pick-up pattern of both units is omni-directional and the frequency response covers the voice and average music range (AM radio or TV sound) with excellent results.

The X-203 (crystal element) has a reasonably flat response from 100 through 7000 cycles per second with an output of —55 db. This is slightly preferable to the B-203 for music pick-up where sensitivity and/or quality under indoor conditions are controlling factors.

The B-203 (ceramic type) also has a reasonably flat response in the range between 100 through 6000 cycles per second with an output level of —62 db. This mike is to be preferred to the crystal where outdoor exposure to high humidity, high temperatures, rough handling or where shock resistance without damage are the most important factors.

Any crystal microphone is a relatively sensitive instrument where

shock, heat and humidity damage are concerned. As the principal element is a crystal of Rochelle salt, extreme humidity can soften it, as can temperatures over 115° F. Crystal microphones should not be stored where they would be subjected to either of these conditions. It is inadvisable, for instance, to put them in such places as the glove compartment or trunk of the car where the temperature can climb to more than 100 degrees in the summertime.

The ceramic type mike would be preferable when children are to operate the recorder where the chances of the mike being dropped or bumped are increased.

The microphone element in both models is shielded and no difficulties were experienced from hum pickup using the length of shielded cord supplied with the mike.

The light weight and small size of these microphones, together with their unobtrusiveness would recommend them for use where microphone concealment is necessary. They should also do well in conjunction with self-contained portables where space is at a premium.

If the mike is used in a concealed position, which necessitates a longer cord than furnished, extension cords should be shielded and grounded to avoid hum and noise pickup. This is true of any high impedance mike.

We found that the specifications of the manufacturer were met or exceeded in all categories of our tests and we feel that either of the microphones is suitable for amateur recording where general area coverage is desired.

Buy American—more mid-1950s mics. (Hi-Fi Tape Recording).

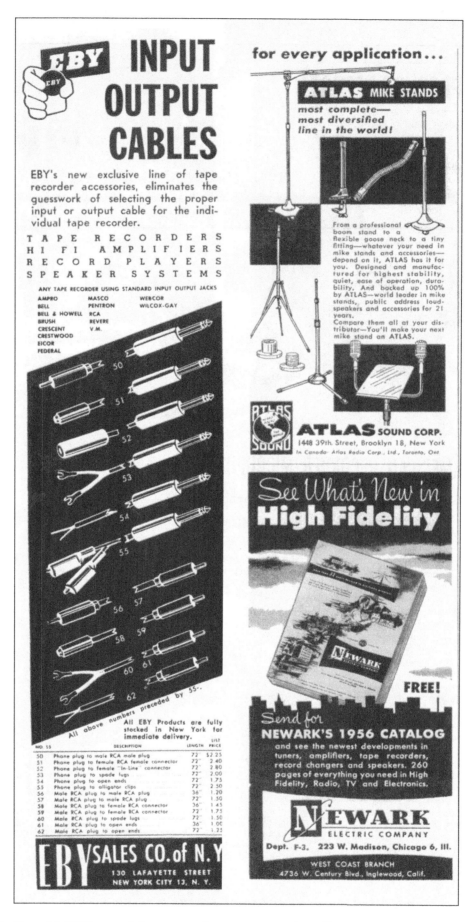
In the mid-1950s, specialty companies were sprouting all over the recording field.

NEW PRODUCT REPORT

MAGNEMITE SELF-CONTAINED
PORTABLE RECORDER

. . . battery operated electronics, spring driven
tape transport, VU meter, broadcast quality.

The all-in-one recorder of the mid-twentieth century.

In this 1958 photo, the 3M Company shows a woman employee packing 10.5 size reel with blank tape. Under the tabletop is an electromagnetic bulk eraser that assures the tape is signal-free.

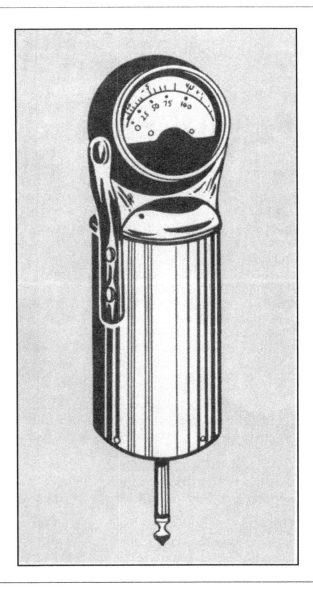

In the early 1950s, audio engineers had a difficult time measuring the correct volume. Then a company named Amplicorp developed a portable VU meter that plugged into the recorder.

Meet **PAUL KLIPSCH**, *pioneer audio engineer and manufacturer*

INSERT — Paul Klipsch at home. His complete sound system includes a Concertone 20/20 and, of course, a Klipschorn, the world-famous speaker that bears his name.

Paul Klipsch with his Concertone at the Santa Monica Airport

"She's never left my side **FOR 27,000 MILES..."**

says **PAUL KLIPSCH** as he boards his Cessna 190 at Santa Monica Airport. His constant companion is a Berlant-Concertone tape recorder. Like the best of traveling companions, it only speaks when spoken to!

Asked why he selects a Concertone Klipsch explains, *"I need a portable recorder that will hold up under rugged treatment. But portability is just one factor Most important to me, the Concertone delivers the full frequency response necessary to demonstrate Klipschorns."*

BERLANT-CONCERTONE *personal choice of leading audio manufacturers*

" You want the same performance, versatility and dependability in a recorder like my friend Paul Klipsch and other audio experts. Trade-up to a Berlant-Concertone professional tape recorder now! THIS MONTH OUR DISTRIBUTORS ARE FEATURING SPECIAL LONG TRADE-IN ALLOWANCES ON THE NEW CONCERTONE TWR-2595. *This complete sound system includes a set of smartly styled portable carrying cases and a matched 10-watt amplifier and extended range speaker. The equivalent sound system with the Berlant Recorder (hysteresis synchronous motor) is specifically designed to meet the needs of the professional recording studios and radio stations "*

BERT BERLANT, President, BERLANT-CONCERTONE

3 REASONS WHY AUDIO EXPERTS USE BERLANT-CONCERTONE RECORDERS

EXCLUSIVE 3 Heads — Provision For 5
Remarkable versatility in use of a single recorder. Separate head for erase, record and playback. Extra heads available for sound-on-sound or stereo recording.

EXCLUSIVE A-B Test Fader
Compare original sound with recorded sound on tape while recording. Set playback volume desired while recording—independent of "Record level."

EXCLUSIVE Simplified Cueing and Editing
Most precise system on any tape recorder for locating exact point on tape and editing.

Concertone TWR-2 – **$445** • Complete sound systems – Concertone TWR-2595 – **$595** • Berlant BRX-1745 – **$745**

WRITE DEPT. 15-N FOR FREE LITERATURE ON PROFESSIONAL TAPE RECORDERS.

Berlant ○ *Concertone* ® *Audio Division of American Electronics Inc., 4917 West Jefferson Blvd., Los Angeles 16, Calif*

EXPORT DIVISION, 232 MADISON AVE., NEW YORK 16, NEW YORK, CABLE: SKYWAVE NEW YORK

For military and industrial requirements, consult: Recordata Division, American Electronics, Inc., 2921 S. Fairfax, L.A. 16, Calif.

Berlant, 1957.

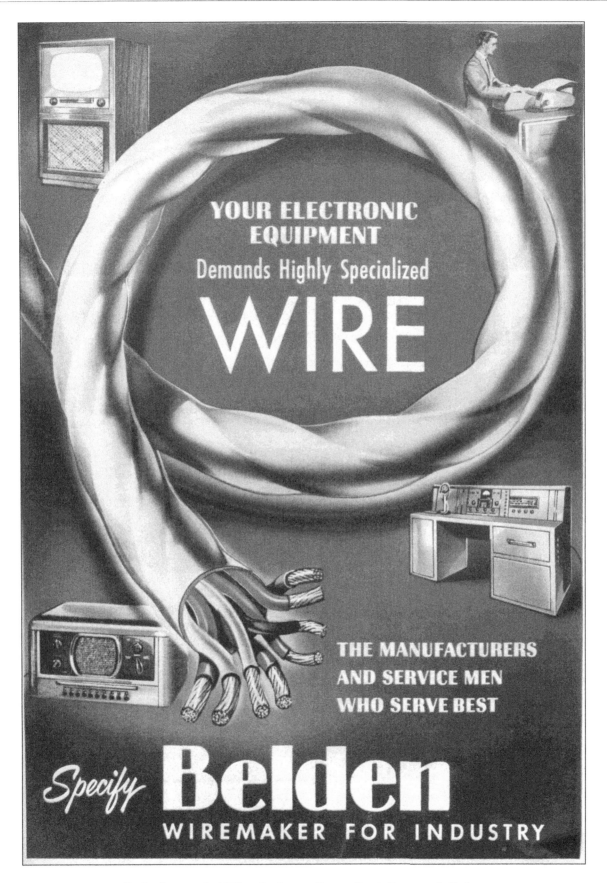

All wired up: early 1950s wire for studios, radio stations, and all places.

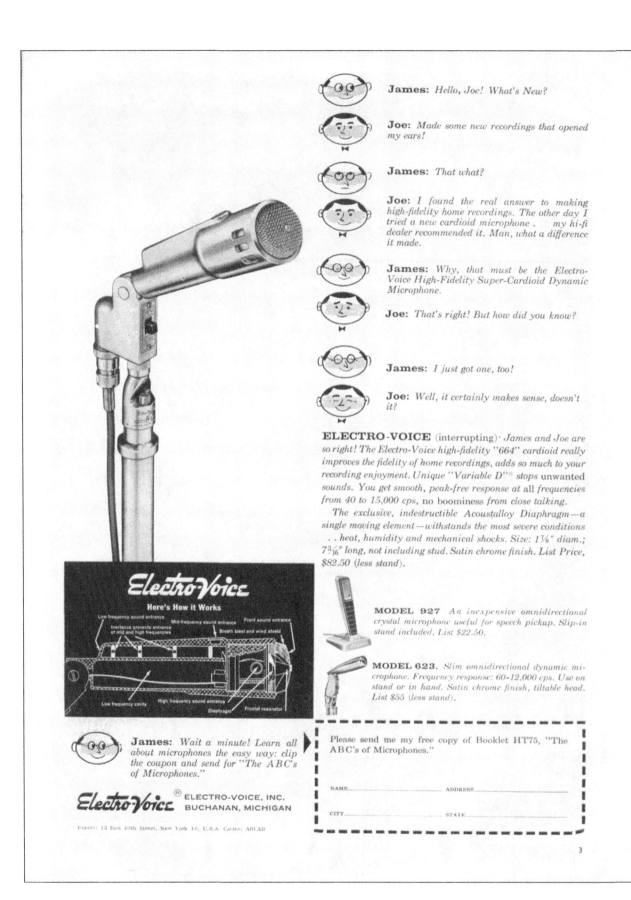

James: *Hello, Joe! What's New?*

Joe: *Made some new recordings that opened my ears!*

James: *That what?*

Joe: *I found the real answer to making high-fidelity home recordings. The other day I tried a new cardioid microphone . my hi-fi dealer recommended it. Man, what a difference it made.*

James: *Why, that must be the Electro-Voice High-Fidelity Super-Cardioid Dynamic Microphone.*

Joe: *That's right! But how did you know?*

James: *I just got one, too!*

Joe: *Well, it certainly makes sense, doesn't it?*

ELECTRO-VOICE (interrupting)· *James and Joe are so right! The Electro-Voice high-fidelity "664" cardioid really improves the fidelity of home recordings, adds so much to your recording enjoyment. Unique "Variable D"® stops unwanted sounds. You get smooth, peak-free response at all frequencies from 40 to 15,000 cps, no boominess from close talking.*

The exclusive, indestructible Acoustalloy Diaphragm—a single moving element—withstands the most severe conditions . . heat, humidity and mechanical shocks. Size: 1⅜" diam.; 7³⁄₁₆" long, not including stud. Satin chrome finish. List Price, $82.50 (less stand).

MODEL 927 *An inexpensive omnidirectional crystal microphone useful for speech pickup. Slip-in stand included. List $22.50.*

MODEL 623. *Slim omnidirectional dynamic microphone. Frequency response: 60-12,000 cps. Use on stand or in hand. Satin chrome finish, tiltable head. List $55 (less stand).*

James: *Wait a minute! Learn all about microphones the easy way: clip the coupon and send for "The ABC's of Microphones."*

Electro-Voice ® ELECTRO-VOICE, INC. BUCHANAN, MICHIGAN

Export: 13 East 40th Street, New York 16, U.S.A. Cables: ARLAB

Please send me my free copy of Booklet HT75, "The ABC's of Microphones."

NAME_____ ADDRESS_____

CITY_____ STATE_____

3

Me: Yes, Electro-Voice was electrifying in 1955.

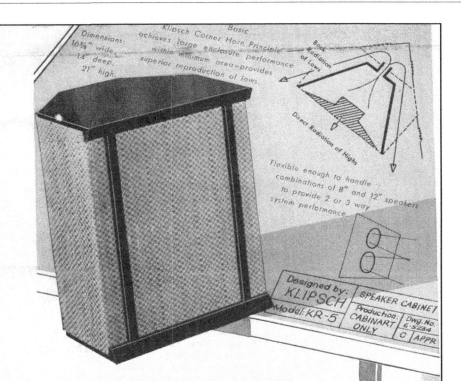

...and the little monster
walked right off
the drawing board!

Conceived in the fertile imagination of Paul Klipsch, America's leading designer of loudspeaker enclosures, and brought to life by the advanced production facilities of CABINART, the Little Monster astounded everyone who came into contact with it. Startled and awed by its almost-Klipschorn performance on light and middle bass, they were amazed at its complete freedom from boom and distortion. You too will be amazed .. **RESPONSE LIKE THIS FROM A 20″ CORNER HORN SPEAKER ENCLOSURE!**

Paul Klipsch had blueprinted a small corner horn enclosure . . . light enough to move anywhere in the home, compact enough to fit in any space, versatile enough to complement any decor, and with performance enough to please the most critical ear . . . thus the Little Monster was born. Size . . . 20 inches; weight . . 28 pounds; versatility . . . it can be wall-mounted, corner-hung, placed on a table, a bench, a shelf, anywhere in the home; performance . . . unbelievable!

The Little Monster, fifth in the Rebel series and thus called the KR-5, approaches Klipschorn performance on light middle bass . . . is excellent for its size even on heavy pipe organ bass. The response is smooth and clean . . . completely free from boom and distortion.

The acoustical science as applied to musical instruments has been incorporated within the Klipsch-Rebel series—so that the enclosure itself assumes the characteristics of a musical reproducer. The KR-5 is thus scientifically engineered to provide the maximum performance possible from a 20″ corner horn.

This latest Klipsch Design by CABINART is available in both finished and Utility (unfinished) models. Also available is a portable model in Leatherette.

Finished $48.00   **Utility $33.00**

See the KR-5 at your local jobber, or write for complete information to Dept. 15-J

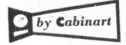

G & H WOOD PRODUCTS CO.,
75 North 11 St., Brooklyn 11, N. Y.

By the late 1950s, speakers were coming out by the dozens.

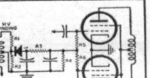
A rectifier sounds rather terrifying. But not to contestants in 1955.

SHE WANTS
FINE FURNITURE

HE WANTS
TECHNICAL EXCELLENCE

YOU SATISFY BOTH WITH

Manfredi

HI-FI SPEAKER ENCLOSURES

HUMMINGBIRD — Model 800 for 8"
speaker; 1200 for 12" speaker. Compact without loss of performance ...
excellent tonal fidelity.

FLAMINGO — Model 2000 — Universal cabinet and speaker enclosure
... maintains high acoustical integrity. Houses complete hi-fi system . .
finest woods and veneers. 36⅛" ×
22¼" × 18½" deep.

You protect your own reputation when you sell a Manfredi
cabinet or enclosure — the
woods stand up...performance
stands out! This excellence has
been the mark of Manfredi
craftsmen for over a quarter-century. Write for illustrated
brochure.

Manfredi
WOOD PRODUCTS CORP.
226 New York Ave., Huntington, L. I., N. Y.

More speakers, 1956.

"Scotch" Brand's <u>dry lubrication</u>

stops magnetic head wear

Enlargement of badly worn and pitted recorder head. Heads in this condition cause loss of high frequency response.

Know what's the most *vulnerable* part of your recorder? It's the sensitive magnetic head—the tiny, precision-made part where dirt or lack of proper lubrication can cause annoying wow, flutter and harmful friction.

It's relatively easy to keep your recorder head free of grime. But how do you keep it well lubricated?

"SCOTCH" Brand Magnetic Tapes do the job for you! *All of these fine tapes are "self-lubricating".* Thanks to "SCOTCH" Brand's exclusive silicone lubrication process, these tapes glide smoothly over the magnetic head. No sticking . . . less friction .. wow and flutter are cut noticeably, even in hot, humid climates!

"SCOTCH" Brand's dry lubrication stays put . . . lasts the life of the tape. And what a difference it makes in the sound of your recordings! You'll *hear* what we mean the next time you play a reel of silicone-lubricated "SCOTCH" Magnetic Tape.

Extra playing time   *Extra strength*   *Higher fidelity*   *True economy*

Your guarantee of <u>quality</u>

<u>only</u> "Scotch" Brand has silicone lubrication

Silicon lubrication was a selling point in 1955.

recording the "man-made moon" on extra-precision audiotape

EARLY in 1958 there will be a "new moon" in the sky — a 22-inch sphere circling the earth at a speed of 18,000 mph. Unlike our real moon, this one will be able to "talk" to Earth. And engineers from Army Ordnance Ballistic Research Laboratories at Aberdeen Proving Ground, Maryland will study these messages to learn new facts about our solar system.

This "moon-talk" — radio signals emanating from precision instruments inside the satellite — is so vital that it will be tape recorded for later analysis, interpretation and preservation.

The highest standards of reproduction must be met. There can be no distortion, voids, or other imperfections.

The tape chosen was extra-precision Type EP Audiotape.

The highest professional standards of quality and uniformity extend throughout the *entire Audiotape line*,

making it the best selection for *any* recording application.

Whether you are an engineer recording highly technical information or a neophyte placing his first reel on a tape recorder, Audiotape will speak for itself. It is now available in *five different types* to meet every recording need and every tape budget. *trademark*

For complete information on the earth satellite recording project write us for a free copy of the December issue of Audio Record.

AUDIO DEVICES, Inc.

444 Madison Avenue, New York 22, N.Y.

Offices in Hollywood — Chicago   Export Dept., 13 E. 40th St., New York, N.Y.

The days of Sputnik and other satellites tied in with audio tape in the late 1950s.

The sound of a bell actually cast by the hands of Paul Revere is recorded at the Dedham Historical Society, Dedham, Mass., by "Woody" Sloan, (left) and Sid Dimond, (right).

Recording the Sounds of Freedom

Radio reporter and engineer record the historic bell in 1956.

Preamp, 1959.

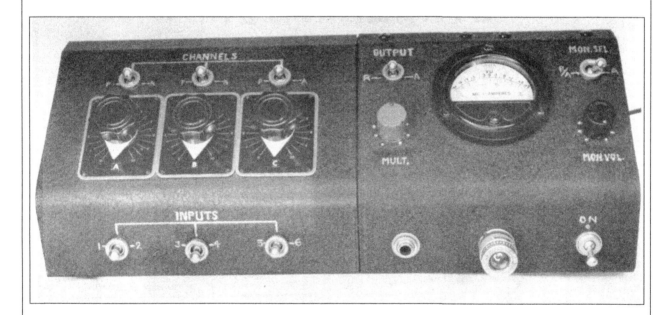

Mixer, early 1950s.

Early stereo attachment, 1955.

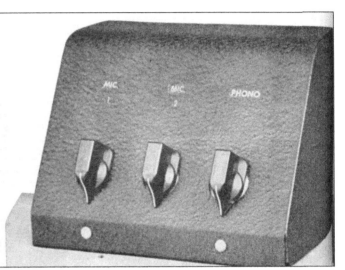

Build this ELECTRONIC MIXER

... with this unit you can mix two microphones and a phonograph.

An early mixer, 1954.

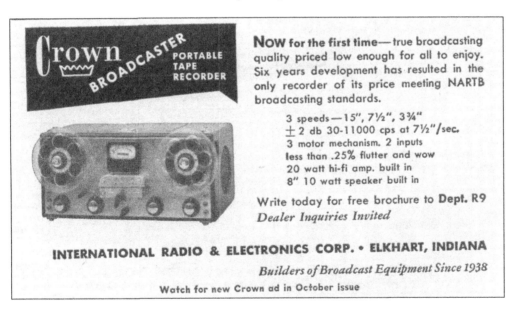

NOW for the first time—true broadcasting quality priced low enough for all to enjoy. Six years development has resulted in the only recorder of its price meeting NARTB broadcasting standards.

3 speeds—15", 7½", 3¾"
± 2 db 30-11000 cps at 7½"/sec.
3 motor mechanism. 2 inputs
less than .25% flutter and wow
20 watt hi-fi amp. built in
8" 10 watt speaker built in

Write today for free brochure to **Dept.** R9
Dealer Inquiries Invited

INTERNATIONAL RADIO & ELECTRONICS CORP. • ELKHART, INDIANA

Builders of Broadcast Equipment Since 1938

Watch for new Crown ad in October issue

A crown portable recorder with professional speed and capabilities, 1956.

INSTANT VISUAL
Selection of all Recordings
ATTA-GLANCE
Approved by Leading Tape & Recorder Mfrs.

Minute scales, indicators, timing tapes are no longer needed. Atta-Glance discs accurately provide perfect timing, editing, indexing, cataloging right on top of the reel for fast, easy reference. Lessens accidental erasure of irreplaceable recordings. Do as Professionals do, save time and money with Atta-Glance Discs.

5" or 7"—8 for only $1.00
Postage Prepaid

TO ENJOY "REEL" PLEASURE WITH YOUR TAPE RECORDER SEND CHECK OR CASH TODAY

Dealer Inquiries Welcomed

HALVICK INDUSTRIES
189 Miller Ave., Mill Valley, Calif.

Recordists in the mid-'50s had their own "high-tech" gizmos.

Engineers in the mid-1950s copy tapes,

experiment with extra tracks, and test new ways to mix sounds.

The magnetic tape that can't be copied!

Others try to imitate it...but no tape equals
SCOTCH 200 Tensilized Double-Length Tape!

This is the original no-break, no-stretch tape that plays twice as long . . and you can't buy better! "SCOTCH" Brand waited until it had perfected an extended play tape of unmatched quality. Now, here it is—"SCOTCH" 200 Tensilized Double-Length Tape—first to give you a Polyester backing with an ultimate tensile strength of 6.8 lbs! And it's the only tape of its kind that offers silicone lubrication, genuine built-in protection for your recorder head. Why settle for imitations when the original and best costs no more? Today, see your dealer for a reel of "SCOTCH" 200 Tensilized Double-Length Tape, newest of the "Tapes you can trust".

No-break, no-stretch became a major selling point in 1956.

An early four-channel mixer, c. 1954.

Top, in these 1958 RCA Victor photos, engineer Ray Hall records in stereo as Ray McClay watches. Below, an engineer runs a master tape that is being copied onto so-called slave tapes.

Build your own isolation booth.

June, 1958   35c

This isolation booth looks like a scene from a '50s sci-fi movie.

Now Showing

The Magnetic War

1948-1958

Wire vs. Tape

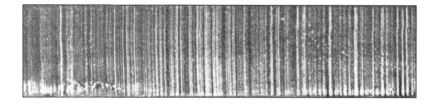

In Memoriam

The Wire Recorder

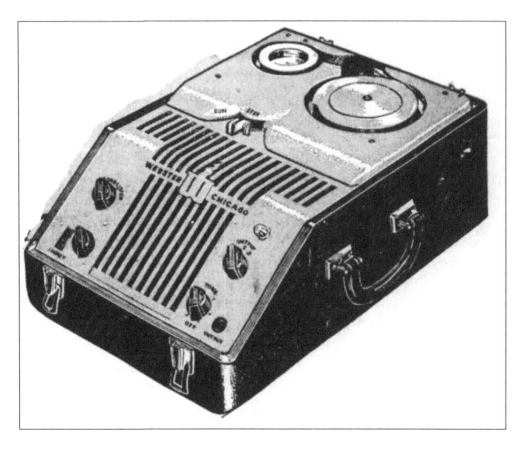

A wire recorder for the home, 1949. Vernon Hornung recorded on one like this.

The Last of the Wire Men

Wire recorders for the public got the jump on tape recorders, starting in earnest as World War II was ending in 1945. The wires would remain popular for ten years for home recording, and to a lesser extent for professional recording in studios and radio stations. Both wire and tape used the magnetic method of storing sound. They were cousins—similar, but decidedly different. Obviously, they could not coexist. You already know the end of the story. Audio tape won the magnetic war. But what you might not know is the story of the wire men.

One of the most popular wire recorders was the Webster-Chicago. It advertised heavily to families through local newspapers. When the Ampex 200 tape recorder arrived on the market in the late 1940s, however, the wire machine was doomed to join the museum of good-ideas-turned-junk. Tape recorders received most of the attention in the media of the day. The home versions were easier to use, and they were a bit more portable. As tape sales boomed, it all seemed like a replay of the invention of the talking machine in the late 1800s.

The battle between wire and tape began in earnest by 1950. A couple of years later, the popularity of wire recorders had declined. But the end had not yet arrived. The battle reminds me of the duel between BETA and VHS, the two types of video recording tape in the 1980s. Once it was clear that VHS recorders had won that war, BETA's days were clearly numbered. It was at that time, about 1984, when I realized I had invested in the wrong side of the war.

So it was with the wire machine. It had its dedicated followers. Sweet memories of it date from my childhood in the early 1950s, when my uncle, Vernon Hornung, bought one specifically to record me. He and my Aunt Claire had no children, so I became Kid Number One. He was fascinated with his new machine, and he learned to record with it quite effectively. He recorded Christmas Eve celebrations, birthday parties, my dad singing, and about anything else my folks did. He also recorded me speaking my first words, singing, telling jokes, and saying silly and serious things. As I grew, he continued to record my words, and later my younger sister's. Because of my early exposure to the wire recorder, I was comfortable in front of the microphone. I knew nothing but the wires. To me, they were synonymous with sound.

About 1951, my aunt and mother started obtaining tickets to Ruth Lyons' *50-50 Club*, shown five days a week on WLWT in Cincinnati. It was the most popular television program in our area. Ruth was the ultimate raconteur and a talented songwriter who composed songs that became local and regional hits, many with a Christmas theme. In 1961, she wrote "Wasn't the Summer Short?," a haunting ballad recorded by Johnny Mathis. Her song "Let's Light the Christmas Tree" was a huge hit in Cincinnati and area cities. Once in those early days, Ruth spotted me in the audience and asked me to join her on her couch, where she chatted about all sorts of subjects. She loved children. I suppose that's why I caught her eye. Even at age three, I was a talker. You could say I was a live wire. Already I was cracking jokes and observing the vagaries of boyhood and automobiles. I told Ruth that I wanted to grow up to own a junkyard. (FYI: I did not fulfill my fantasy.) Ruth and her sidekick, Willie Thall, also a songwriter and emcee of the station's *Midwestern Hayride*, loved exploring my tiny mind. Every time my mother and aunt returned to visit the show, Ruth would say, "Randy's back! Come on up here!" Back at home on my TV-star days, my uncle always got away from his job as a butcher to record me with his wire machine as I held court on the airwaves. Then in the early 1960s, pre-adolescence intervened. I became too awkward and shy to talk much while visiting Ruth's show. My little sister stepped in. I preferred to walk around WLWT with one of Ruth's staff members, watching the big tape recorders' reels spin.

It was about this time that my uncle strayed. He went out and bought a used Revere tape recorder. It wasn't much lighter, but it looked more futuristic to me. I noticed that he never really took to it, and at my urging he gave it to me. He didn't mind. He was a *wire* man to the core of the spool. Wire men just looked at tape recorders and sighed.

In what must have seemed a blink of his eyes, I grew up. He kept those little spools of wire for a half-century, until they began to snap when played. They flew like tiny whips as the spool spun uncontrollably. This upset him, but he figured he had gotten his money's worth. The wires had proved to be as durable as tapes, and just as clear-sounding. To rescue their deteriorating sounds, he spent the 1990s laboriously copying the survivors to audio cassettes. He thought at least that medium would stick around. He enjoyed sitting at the kitchen table in his old house, often reliving the days when wire was king and I was a junkyard owner-in-waiting. By then, Aunt Claire was gone. So were my mother and father. Ruth had retired long ago, and shortly thereafter she died, grieving over the death of her young daughter. Uncle Vernon looked around and realized he was the last of the people I had loved since those days of Ruth's show.

Sadly, my uncle and first recording engineer died in 2004 at age ninety-three. On a cold, gray day in February, a few days after his death, I lugged his heavy old Webster-Chicago home with me, with dozens of spools I found in a wooden box he had made to hold them all. Carrying our family's good times, those thin wires would become like ancient texts lost in a cave, waiting to be discovered by a future generation. As I looked at the recorder, and held the spools in my hands, I grieved for something that had died with him. I realized that I was now the keeper of the wires of our lives. Now, I was the last one. I managed to smile, for now I had become the last of the wire men.

In the late 1940s, Webster-Chicago promoted its wire recorders by advertising extensively in local newspapers. One advertisement consisted of a newspaper page, complete with stories.

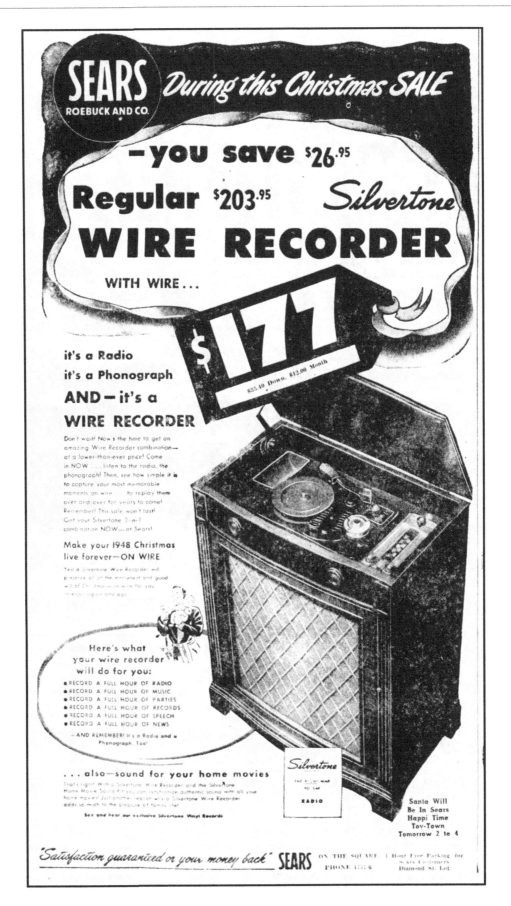

In 1948, when Sears and wire were kings, you could buy a fancy cabinet recorder.

By 1948, the magnetic wire recorder seemed invincible. Then came magnetic tape.

Another wire recorder, from 1950.

Another how-to book on magnetic recording, 1954.

by PRECISION AUDIO PRODUCTS Inc.

PROFESSIONAL HIGH FIDELITY WIRE RECORDER

40 — 10,000 Cycles

Designed To Fulfill
Every Professional
And Broadcast
Requirement!

$295.50

Complete with 1 half-hour spool
and 2 quarter-hour spools of
wire. Less microphone.

AMONG THE FEATURES OF THE WIREMASTER:

- Never before a recorder like the Wiremaster, the last word in sound reproducing instruments, and truly a quality unit to satisfy the most discriminating professional user. A wide frequency range (40-10,000 cps) and extremely low noise level are among the many exclusive features that have been combined to reproduce both speech and music so faithfully as to actually duplicate the quality of the original sound.

- Two high-impedance microphone inputs, each with its own mixing and fading control.

- Built-in broadcast band radio with better-than-average quality, which can be used for radio-recording, air checks, etc.

- Play-back arm for playing discs up to 12" You may record directly from disc to wire.

- Full frequency reproduction is accomplished with separate bass and treble controls for boost or attenuation on all channels.

- Speaker monitoring control enables you to adjust *listening* volume to your own comfort without affecting *recording* volume, which is regulated by a separate control.

- 13 tube circuit (including rectifier) with push-pull 6V6 output, plays through high fidelity, 8", extended range speaker, housed in separate baffle to avoid vibration and accoustical feedback.

- Dubbing Jack for recording directly from wire to discs.

- Entirely self-contained and portable.

Wiremaster company made a professional model of the wire recorder in the late 1940s. It featured a speed of 24 IPS. Unfortunately for the company, wire recorders did not catch on with professional users as much as taper recorders did.

OTHER FEATURES WHICH MAKE THE WIREMASTER
THE RECORDER FOR *PROFESSIONAL* USE

● High fidelity, triple-action head records, plays back immediately, and erases automatically when new recording is made. You may delete undesired sections of a recorded broadcast without affecting the rest of it. Exclusive construction of head eliminates hum, extends frequency range.

● Wire may be "edited" by merely cutting off undesired sections of wire and knotting the remaining ends together. These knots will not be heard in playback.

● All controls are located on the front panel, and plainly marked for fool-proof operation. The Wiremaster is simple to operate.

● All channels may be intermixed, enabling you to record your voice with the radio or phonograph, or to speak into microphone while wire is playing back. (See specifications for channels.)

● External phonograph input enables recording directly onto wire from an external source, such as FM tuner or transcription turntable.

● Vibrations will not affect recording.

● Wire may be replayed thousands of times with no loss of fidelity or increase of noise. Available in 15 minute, 30 minute, and 1 hour spools.

A Word About Its Exclusive Wire-Moving Features

An entirely new principle of wire-movement in the Wiremaster prevents tangling and breaking, and accomplishes professional "flutter-free" wire movement and smooth, even spooling. Spools automatically shut off when either one completely unwinds. Up to 1 hour continuous recording on a spool of wire.

As the Wiremaster has separate motors for play and rewind, as well as all-electronic switching, the direction of the moving wire may be reversed as rapidly as possible without breakage. Rewind is at an 8:1 ratio.

ADDITIONAL WIRE:

1 hour spool $5.00	½ hour spool $3.00
¼ hour spool $2.00	Empty spool ....$ .45

TECHNICAL SPECIFICATIONS

Frequency Response
40-10,000 cycles per second.

Noise Level
—70 DB.

Wire Speed
24″ per second.

Rewind
8:1 ratio.

Motors
Separate, heavy duty, fully cased motors for forward play and rewind.

Channels
2 high impedance microphones.
1 external phonograph or tuner.
Self-contained superheterodyne radio.
Built-in phonograph.

Gain
Microphone channels, 130 DB.
Phonograph, 90 DB.

Tone Equalizers
+10 DB, —15 DB at 10,000 cps.
+8 DB, — 17 DB at 100 cps.

Power Output
5 Watts undistorted. 8ohm output jack on panel.

Controls
Microphone 1, Microphone 2, Playback Gain, Bass, Treble, Speaker Volume, Record-Listen-Rewind Switch, Radio-Phono Switch, Radio Volume, Radio Tuning, On-Off Switch.

Dubbing Jack
Output ½ Volt. All tone equalizers in circuit. Output: high impedance.

Tubes
2-6SJ7, 1-6SC7, 3-6SL7GT, 3-6V6GT, 1-6SK7, 1-6SA7, 1-6SQ7, 1-5U4G.

Volume Indicators
2 neon volume level indicators, one for Normal, and one for Overload.

Fuse
3 Amperes.

Power Supply
105-120 Volts, 60 cycles.

Linecord
10 feet, heavy rubber.

Speaker
Extended Range, High Fidelity, 8″, PM speaker, housed in separate baffle. Speaker cord, 10 feet.

Case
Portable, two-tone, durable leatherette, with leather reinforced corners. 2 locks.

Size
23″ x 15″ x 12″.

Weight
49 lbs. complete.

AVAILABLE AT:

NEW ADDRESS

SONOCRAFT CO., Inc.
45 WEST 45th STREET   NEW YORK 19, N. Y.

Telephone: BRyant 9-8997-8

Technical specifications for the Wiremaster.

In 1950, Webster-Chicago was making wire recorders and phonographs. It was selling what Is advertised as a "semi-professional wire recorder," for serious recordists. Below, a competitor, the Pierce Wire Recorder.

SALES TERRITORY AVAILABLE
FOR
PEIRCE
WIRE RECORDER

Sensational Dictation Machine

Representatives of the Peirce Wire Recorder Corp. will be at the Bond Hotel August 14 and 15, to interview applicants for distributorship in Hartford and trading area. Exclusive franchise for those interested in exclusive sales of Peirce Wire Recorder. Must be financially responsible.

**Write to John E. Bogan or
Telephone Hotel Bond
For Appointment**

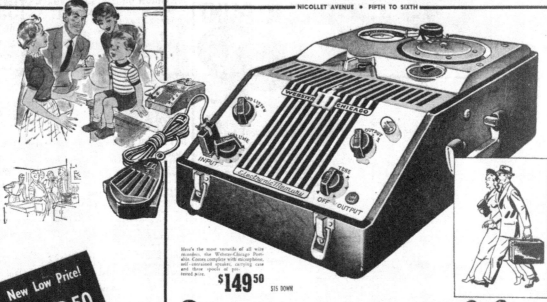

Silvertone Wire Recorder Combination

199⁵⁰

Complete with mike and one full hour spool of wire all set to record.

EASY TERMS

It's a glorious, super sensitive radio that makes radio programs sparkle with zest. It's a smoothie of a phonograph with a crystal pickup that is as sensitive as a kitten . . . and it's a full hour wire recorder that will make your eyes pop with delight. Records as you listen. It has a world of uses . . . fun in the home . . . educational in schools . . . efficiency in business . . . because it records for one full hour on one small spool of 7500 feet of stainless steel wire, so compact that it fits in the palm of your hand. permanent, lasts forever . . . or easily erased, simply record over the old recording. No discs, no needles, no shavings, no warping . . . can be played back immediately.

WIRE RECORDER SPOOL
Records an hour's entertainment. **4.95** 7500 feet

IV.

More Victorious Tape Machines

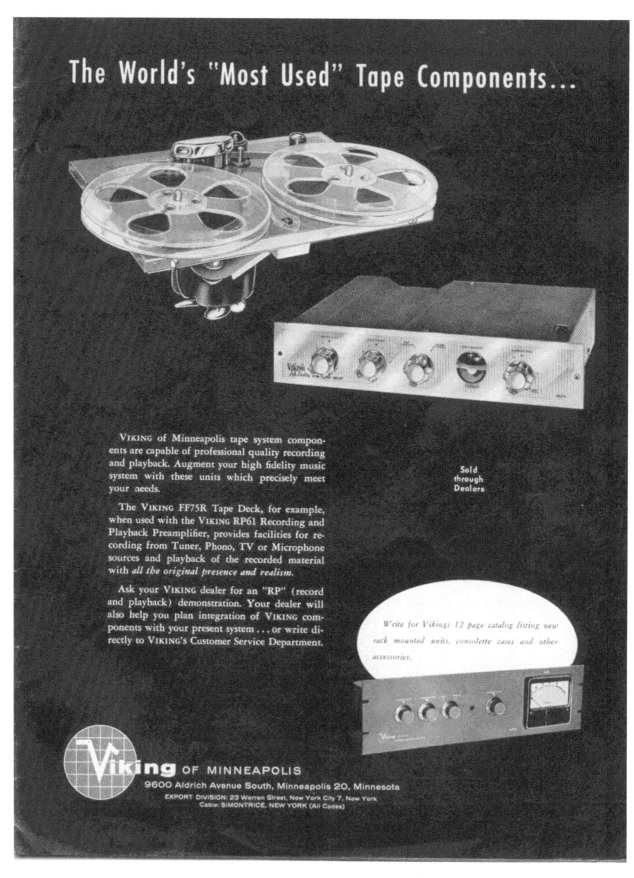

In 1957, another Minnesota sound giant, Viking, offered its catalog of new products to tape recorder users, both pro and amateur.

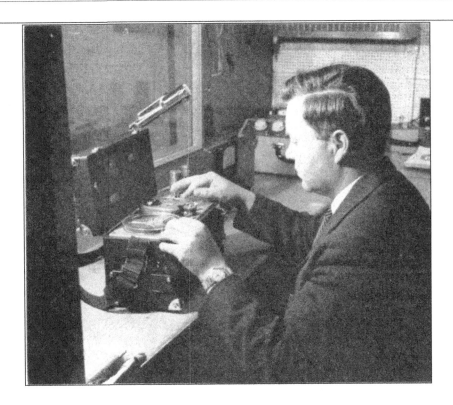

Mike Roberts, program director of CHUM Radio in Toronto, helped build a small studio at the station to record programs in 1959. Prior to that, the station recorded on a Revere T1100 with two crystal mics. After the studio was built, Roberts acquired an EMI L2B recorder. Below, in 1959 an audio engineer from the States prepares to operate his studio's two-track recorder.

Ampex shows off its latest speaker, 1959.

Revere's exclusive *Balanced Tone* makes the difference

in the brilliant high fidelity of

Revere TAPE RECORDERS

The incomparable high fidelity and rich tonal quality of Revere Tape Recorders is the direct result of a Revere exclusive, patented feature. "Balanced-Tone" is the control that coordinates amplifier and acoustic system response to emphasize both high and low tones, giving strikingly realistic HIGH FIDELITY sound reproduction, even on low volume. Compare and you'll choose REVERE!

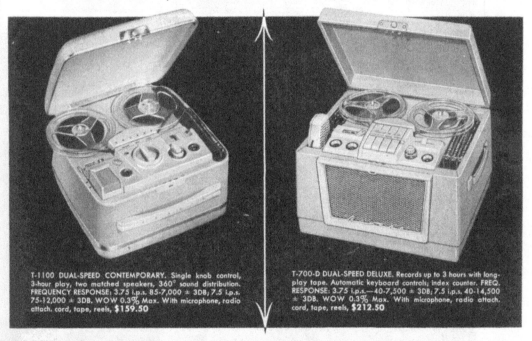

T-1100 DUAL-SPEED CONTEMPORARY. Single knob control, 3-hour play, two matched speakers, 360° sound distribution. FREQUENCY RESPONSE: 3.75 i.p.s. 85-7,000 ± 3DB; 7.5 i.p.s. 75-12,000 ± 3DB. WOW 0.3% Max. With microphone, radio attach. cord, tape, reels, **$159.50**

T-700-D DUAL-SPEED DELUXE. Records up to 3 hours with long-play tape. Automatic keyboard controls; index counter. FREQ. RESPONSE: 3.75 i.p.s.—40-7,500 ± 3DB; 7.5 i.p.s. 40-14,500 ± 3DB. WOW 0.3% Max. With microphone, radio attach. cord, tape, reels, **$212.50**

Announcing

REVERE T-11 CUSTOM RECORDER

For professional use and custom home installation. Accurate 7.5 i.p.s. tape speed. Solenoid operated keyboard push-button control. Revere patented automatic head demagnetization. Two-level recording indicator. Index counter. Accepts 3, 5, 7 and 10½-inch reels. Monitor amplifier with 2½ watt output; cathode follower output. 2200 ohms at 1 volt. With reel adapters and plugs $264.50

FREQ. RESP. 40-16,000 ± 3DB
WOW AND FLUTTER less than 0.2%

The preference for Revere by artists of renown is your guide to recorder selection.

REVERE CAMERA COMPANY • CHICAGO 16, ILLINOIS

ARTUR RUBINSTEIN *noted pianist* | **MARIAN ANDERSON** *famed soprano* | **ANDRES SEGOVIA** *foremost guitarist* | **ZINO FRANCESCATTI** *brilliant violinist* | **ROBERT CASADESUS** *piano virtuoso* | **LAURITZ MELCHIOR** *great Wagnerian tenor*

5

Revere was a big name in recorders in the mid-1950s. The company was known primarily for its home-market recorders. The author's first full-size recorder was the Revere T-700-Dual, pictured above. His came via his uncle—twenty years after it was made.

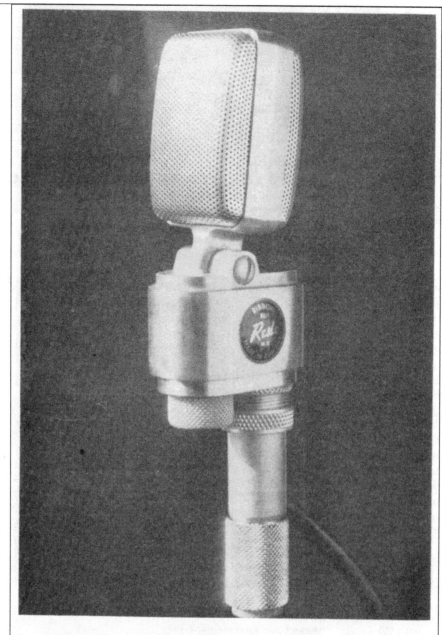

RESLO RIBBON MICROPHONE

. . . a tough little microphone with excellent characteristics for recording or PA work.

A new microphone arrives in 1959.

Are you a recording engineer?

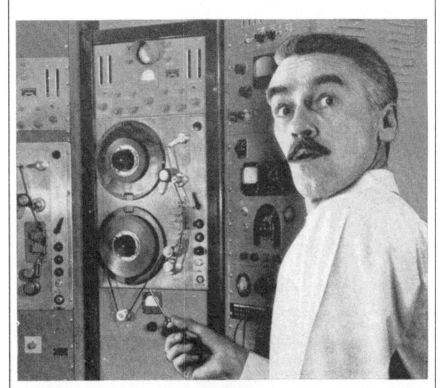

"No, I'm a plumber

...but I know good recording tape"

AUDIOTAPE, the thinking recordist's tape, gives you the full, rich reproduction so satisfying to the happy audiophile — be he doctor, lawyer or Indian chief. Because behind every reel of Audiotape are two decades of research and development in sound recording.

When you buy a reel of Audiotape you're getting the tape that's the professionals' choice. Why? For example, the machines that coat the oxides onto the base material are unique in this field — designed and built by Audio engineers who couldn't find commercial machines that met their rigid specifications. Then there's the C-slot reel — the fastest-threading reel ever developed. For that matter, there's the oxide itself — blended and combined with a special binder that eliminates oxide rub-off.

There are many more reasons why the professionals insist on Audiotape. They know that there is only one quality of Audiotape. And this single top quality standard is maintained throughout each reel, and from reel to reel — for all eight types of Audiotape. That's what makes Audiotape the world's finest magnetic recording tape. For recording engineers, doctors, garbage men, investment brokers, sculptors and plumbers!

Manufactured by AUDIO DEVICES, INC.
444 Madison Ave., New York 22, New York
Offices in Hollywood & Chicago

This actor appeared in several Audiotape advertisements in 1959.

A Turner mic, 1959.

Welcome to the big show! Recordists see it all in the fall of '57.

Pentron CA-14, 4-channel mixer with 6 high impedance inputs: 4 microphone, 2 phono (phono input receptacles are on rear of unit; microphone inputs are on front panel); provides 8 db gain in microphone channels. Tubes are 2—12AX7.

Masco model EMM-6 electronic mixer-pre-amplifier has six inputs (4 microphone and 2 phono). Three 12AX7 tubes, selenium rectifier. Cathode follower output—allows 400-foot separation from amplifier; any four channels are separately controlled.

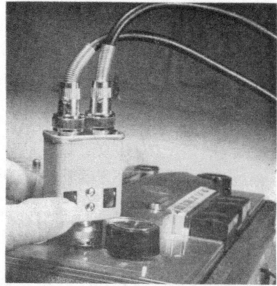

Switchcraft "Mini-Mix," a miniature 2-input audio mixer. Accommodates two high impedance inputs; resistance type mixer. Separate gain controls, recessed inside housing. Brown finished case, nickel plated accessories.

Mixers and pre-amps from 1959.
(Courtesy *Hi-Fi Tape Recording*)

AMPEX SERIES 300 TAPE RECORDERS

for master recording

AMPEX
CORPORATION
*professional
products division*

Three tracks! Ampex break down the long-held two-track wall. With three, engineers and producers to add more "sweetening" to their masters. Those used to working on one- and two-track machines were awed by the advance, but it didn't last long. Soon the four-track recorder would become the latest innovation.

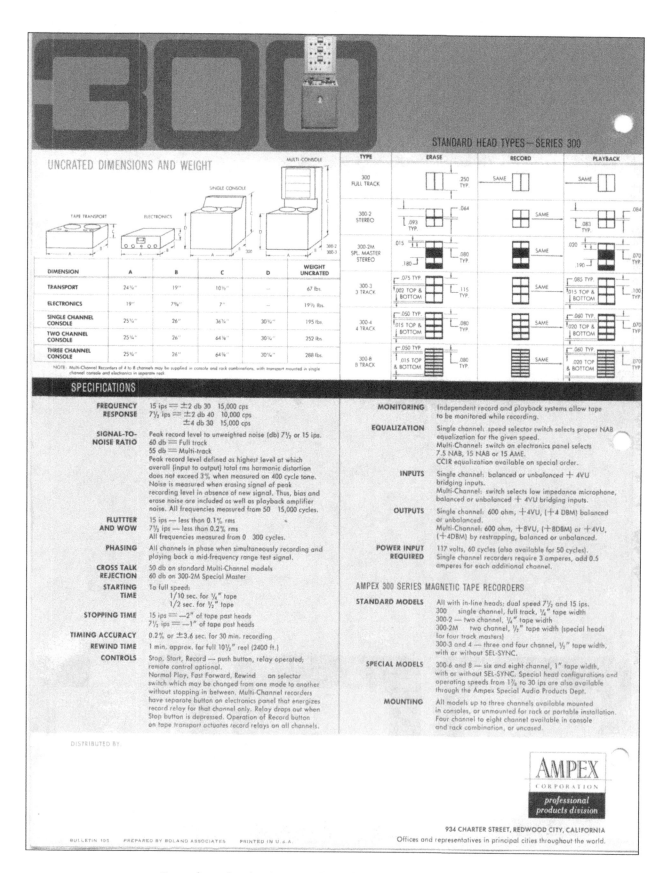

300

STANDARD HEAD TYPES — SERIES 300

TYPE	ERASE	RECORD	PLAYBACK
300 FULL TRACK	.250 TYP.	SAME	SAME
300-2 STEREO	.093 TYP. / .064	SAME	.083 TYP. / .084
300-2M SPL. MASTER STEREO	.015 / .180 / .080 TYP.	SAME	.020 / .190 / .070 TYP.
300-3 3 TRACK	.075 TYP. / .002 TOP & BOTTOM / .115 TYP.	SAME	.085 TYP. / .015 TOP & BOTTOM / .100 TYP.
300-4 4 TRACK	.050 TYP. / .015 TOP & BOTTOM / .080 TYP.	SAME	.060 TYP. / .020 TOP & BOTTOM / .070 TYP.
300-8 8 TRACK	.050 TYP. / .015 TOP & BOTTOM / .080 TYP.	SAME	.060 TYP. / .020 TOP & BOTTOM / .070 TYP.

UNCRATED DIMENSIONS AND WEIGHT

DIMENSION	A	B	C	D	WEIGHT UNCRATED
TRANSPORT	24¼"	19"	10½"	—	67 lbs.
ELECTRONICS	19"	7⅝"	7"	—	19½ lbs.
SINGLE CHANNEL CONSOLE	25¼"	26"	36¼"	30¼"	195 lbs.
TWO CHANNEL CONSOLE	25¼"	26"	64⅛"	30¼"	252 lbs
THREE CHANNEL CONSOLE	25¼"	26"	64⅛"	30¼"	288 lbs

NOTE: Multi-Channel Recorders of 4 to 8 channels may be supplied in console and rack combinations, with transport mounted in single channel console and electronics in separate rack.

SPECIFICATIONS

FREQUENCY RESPONSE
15 ips = ±2 db 30 — 15,000 cps
7½ ips = ±2 db 40 — 10,000 cps
±4 db 30 — 15,000 cps

SIGNAL-TO-NOISE RATIO
Peak record level to unweighted noise (db) 7½ or 15 ips.
60 db = Full track
55 db = Multi-track
Peak record level defined as highest level at which overall (input to output) total rms harmonic distortion does not exceed 3% when measured on 400 cycle tone. Noise is measured when erasing signal of peak recording level in absence of new signal. Thus, bias and erase noise are included as well as playback amplifier noise. All frequencies measured from 50 — 15,000 cycles.

FLUTTTER AND WOW
15 ips — less than 0.1% rms
7½ ips — less than 0.2% rms
All frequencies measured from 0 — 300 cycles.

PHASING
All channels in phase when simultaneously recording and playing back a mid-frequency range test signal.

CROSS TALK REJECTION
50 db on standard Multi-Channel models
60 db on 300-2M Special Master

STARTING TIME
To full speed:
1/10 sec. for ¼" tape
1/2 sec. for ½" tape

STOPPING TIME
15 ips = —2" of tape past heads
7½ ips = —1" of tape past heads

TIMING ACCURACY
0.2% or ±3.6 sec. for 30 min. recording

REWIND TIME
1 min. approx. for full 10½" reel (2400 ft.)

CONTROLS
Stop, Start, Record — push button, relay operated; remote control optional.
Normal Play, Fast Forward, Rewind — on selector switch which may be changed from one mode to another without stopping in between. Multi-Channel recorders have separate button on electronics panel that energizes record relay for that channel only. Relay drops out when Stop button is depressed. Operation of Record button on tape transport actuates record relays on all channels.

MONITORING
Independent record and playback systems allow tape to be monitored while recording.

EQUALIZATION
Single channel: speed selector switch selects proper NAB equalization for the given speed.
Multi-Channel: switch on electronics panel selects 7.5 NAB, 15 NAB or 15 AME.
CCIR equalization available on special order.

INPUTS
Single channel: balanced or unbalanced + 4VU bridging inputs.
Multi-Channel: switch selects low impedance microphone, balanced or unbalanced + 4VU bridging inputs.

OUTPUTS
Single channel: 600 ohm, +4VU, (+4 DBM) balanced or unbalanced.
Multi-Channel: 600 ohm, +8VU, (+8DBM) or +4VU, (+4DBM) by restrapping, balanced or unbalanced.

POWER INPUT REQUIRED
117 volts, 60 cycles (also available for 50 cycles).
Single channel recorders require 3 amperes, add 0.5 amperes for each additional channel.

AMPEX 300 SERIES MAGNETIC TAPE RECORDERS

STANDARD MODELS
All with in-line heads; dual speed 7½ and 15 ips.
300 — single channel, full track, ¼" tape width
300-2 — two channel, ¼" tape width
300-2M — two channel, ½" tape width (special heads for four track masters)
300-3 and 4 — three and four channel, ½" tape width, with or without SEL-SYNC.

SPECIAL MODELS
300-6 and 8 — six and eight channel, 1" tape width, with or without SEL-SYNC. Special head configurations and operating speeds from 1⅞ to 30 ips are also available through the Ampex Special Audio Products Dept.

MOUNTING
All models up to three channels available mounted in consoles, or unmounted for rack or portable installation. Four channel to eight channel available in console and rack combination, or uncased.

DISTRIBUTED BY:

AMPEX
CORPORATION
professional products division

934 CHARTER STREET, REDWOOD CITY, CALIFORNIA
Offices and representatives in principal cities throughout the world.

BULLETIN 105   PREPARED BY BOLAND ASSOCIATES   PRINTED IN U.S.A.

Spec sheet for the Ampex 300 series recorder, three tracks.

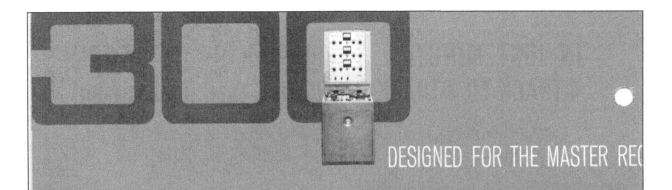

DESIGNED FOR THE MASTER REC

WIDE RANGE RECORDING

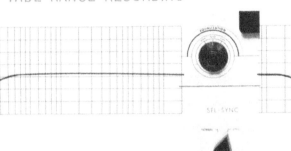

Negligible flutter and wow The requirements of the professional recording market — wherein the ultimate consumer may get up to the sixth generation recording — make it imperative that the master tape be free from flutter and wow. This can only be achieved through the Ampex 300 Recorders whose flutter and wow characteristics are so low as to be practically eliminated. Even when pyramided through several generations, flutter and wow are still far too insignificant to be audible.

Frequency response Combining an essentially flat response from 30 to 15,000 cycles with a high signal-to-noise ratio, and the almost complete freedom from flutter and wow, results in master recordings of unsurpassed quality. And — Ampex Series 300 Recorders continue to deliver this ultimate in performance even after many years of continuous use.

Three equalizations NAB equalization is supplied on single channel models unless otherwise ordered. Multi-Channel versions are supplied with exclusive AME (Ampex Master Equalization) and NAB as standard equipment; CCIR equalization can also be ordered. The AME curve represents a considerable advance in master recording and gives an effective 7 db increase in signal-to-noise ratio over the 2,000 to 6,000 cycle range — thus reducing "subjective" tape hiss found in this frequency range. This lower noise level is particularly advantageous in producing the new 4-track stereo tapes.

Monitoring An AB switch allows comparison of input and tape output by means of (1) a VU meter, (2) headphones plugged into the front panel, or by (3) a line connected to the studio monitor circuit.

TAPE TRANSPORT

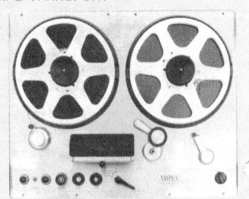

Tape transport Three precision, heavy duty motors handle reels up to 14 inches in diameter, tapes up to 1 inch in width (the Ampex Series 300 are the only recorders that will accommodate more than one-half inch tape). Flutter and wow have been virtually eliminated due to rigid unit assembly, carefully designed precision capstan drive, massive flywheel and longer tape path. Tape skewing is non-existent; starts and stops are instantaneous.

Controls Record, Start and Stop buttons are recessed so that they will not be accidentally pressed; all can be remote controlled. A Fast Start/Slow Start switch allows the capstan motor to remain in "on" or "standby" position.

Long-life precision heads The rugged construction and carefully controlled fabrication assures uniform characteristics during their exceptionally long life. Ampex magnetic heads tested after 15,000 to 18,000 operating hours still meet published specifications in virtually every instance.

Precision Alignment Ampex Multi-Channel recorders add an additional element of quality; the precision manufacture and alignment of the Multi-Channel heads. They are so perfect, so uniform, that tapes recorded on an Ampex Multi-Channel can be played with perfect results on any other Ampex Multi-Channel anywhere in the world without phase shift between channels.

More information about the three-track machine.

IN JUST MINUTES . . . YOU CAN SWITCH FROM 4-TRACK TO 3-TRACK RECORDING (and back again!)

with the SCULLY 282-4 recorder/reproducer...

and interchangeable plug-in three track heads

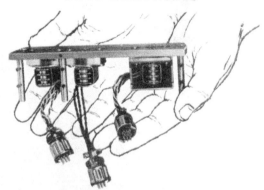

HERE'S THE STORY: Buy the SCULLY 282-4 for 4-track, ½" recording and you get the finest solid-state instrument available built to the exacting standards of craftsmanship and performance for which the SCULLY name is so well known. Expect sound performance unequalled dependability in the most critical and demanding applications.

NOW add this 3-channel head assembly which plugs in and converts the SCULLY 282-4 to a 3-track unit. Gives you just the flexibility you're looking for, doesn't it?

HOW MUCH?

SCULLY 282-4 (unmounted)	$3945.00
3-channel, plug-in head assembly	586.00
	$4531.00

USERS ARE SAYING:

"   Scully 280 out-performs all our other machines."

> Dave Bofils
> Gotham Recording, N.Y.C.

"Head interchangeability has doubled value of our half-inch Scully."

> Ed Green
> Edgewood Recording, Washington, D.C.

"   azimuth alignment between 3 and 4 track assemblies is excellent!"

> Paul Friedberger
> Associated Recording, N.Y.C.

"   three/four track Scully produces our best tapes."

> Bill Stahl
> Ultra Sonic, N.Y.

TECHNICAL DATA:

FREQUENCY RESPONSE: ±2 db 30 to 18,000 cps @ 15 ips; ±2 db 50 to 15,000 cps @ 7½ ips; ±2 db 50 to 7500 cps @ 3¾ ips

SIGNAL TO NOISE RATIO: Peak record to unweighted noise (50 to 15,000 cps band) using 3M 201 or equivalent tape

7½ and 15 ips full track	—65 db
7½ and 15 ips stereo	—60 db
3¾ ips full track	—55 db

FLUTTER AND WOW:

15 ips:	Better than 0.08% RMS
7½ ips:	Better than 0.1% RMS
3¾ ips:	Better than 0.2% RMS

SCRAPE:

15 ips:	Better than 0.12%
7½ ips:	Better than 0.15%

(All components 300 to 5,000 cps)

JUST A WORD MORE about SCULLY all-transistor recording equipment. It has an outstanding operational record   insuring minimum down-time during sessions. When servicing is required, its plug-in construction makes for fast, easy repair Relays, modular sub-assemblies, electronic chassis, solid-state amplifiers all **plug in**   no complicated wiring disconnects or de-soldering.

CALL 203-335-5146
or WRITE US

SCULLY RECORDING INSTRUMENTS CORP.

480 BUNNELL STREET, BRIDGEPORT, CONN.

TEL. (203) 335-5146

Scully goes four track—circa 1967. Some great records would be cut on four tracks, including some by the Beatles and the Beach Boys.

Breakthrough! Eight tracks arrive. This machine is from Scully, a major name in recorders. Eight-track machines were invading the market by the late 1960s and into 1970. They were top of the line in studio recorders until the new sixteen-track models came on the scene in the early 1970s. As the old saying goes, What have you done for me today, not yesterday.

Scully Model 284-8

Eight channel one inch master tape recorder/reproducer mounted in walnut Formica console mount.

Frequency Response

± 2 db 30 to 18,000 Hz @ 30 ips
± 2 db 30 to 15,000 Hz @ 15 ips
+ 2 db - 3 db 50 to 15,000 Hz @ 7½ ips

Signal to Noise Ratio

Peak record level to noise using 3M 202 tape or equivalent
30 ips   - 63 db
7½ & 15 ips - 62 db
Unweighted, 30 - 18,000 Hz band

Flutter & wow

30 ips 0.06% RMS
15 ips 0.08% RMS
7½ ips 0.1% RMS

Price, f.o.b. Bridgeport, Conn. $11,850

EIGHT CHANNEL

Scully Sync/master®

New remote sync switching unit with new flexibility and ease for modern recording sync techniques. Includes remote automatic tape filter defeat for easier cueing plus all standard remote functions.

Price, f.o.b. Bridgeport, Conn. $1,095

THE SCULLY TRADITION

Scully disc recording equipment has been the standard of precision and quality throughout the world for more than 48 years. All Scully tape recorders and reproducers are designed and built with the same high degree of craftsmanship as the famous Scully Lathes. The Model 280 Series represents an important advance in the state of the art. It is indispensable in critical audio applications where exacting performance is a requirement.

Specs for the Scully eight-track recorder.

Though it didn't roll at 15 IPS, the Ampex 600 was a fine recorder that some producers used to record demos and live performances. This model is from 1955.

STEREO WEBCOR

All-new 1959 Webcor Stereofonic Tape Recorders outperform the field!

Never before has Webcor offered such a wide variety of both stereo and monaural tape recorders. New Webcor Stereofonic Tape Recorders play back recorded stereo tapes with unmatched realism   record and play back monaurally. They're packed with the kind of exclusives and advantages you've been waiting for!

See and hear the new 1959 Webcor Tape Recorders at your dealer's now!

Regent Stereofonic Tape Recorder—Model 2820—The featherweight marvel in the stereo tape recorder field! Plays in vertical or horizontal position—stereofonic playback—three speed operation for monaural record and playback—power amplifier and stereo pre-amplifier—wide-range 5″ x 7″ PM speaker—edit key—Webcor-built recording head—Ext. Amplifier, Ext. Speaker, Input provisions. Ebony Designed for use with 3-Speaker Stereo Sound System, Model 4820 (optional).

Royal Stereofonic Tape Recorder—Model 2821—New 1959 stereo version of the world's most popular tape recorder! Stereofonic playback—"no reel-turnover" feature for monaural record and playback—powerful amplifier and stereo pre-amplifier—one 5″ x 7″ woofer, one 4″ tweeter —co-linear (stacked) stereo playback heads—automatic shut-off—Ext. Amplifier, Ext. Speaker, Input provisions. Ebony or White. For use with 3-Speaker Stereo Sound System, Model 4820 (optional).

LISTEN! ALL MUSIC SOUNDS BETTER ON A WEBCOR!

A BAKER'S DOZEN HIGHLY INFLUENTIAL INDIE RECORDING STUDIOS OF THE TAPE-RECORDING ERA

*Based on personal opinion, hit records, clout, and
cultural contributions to their communities and regions.**

1. UNIVERSAL STUDIOS, Chicago, 1950s-1960s.
2. BELL SOUND, New York, 1950s-1960s.
3. A&R RECORDING, New York, 1960s-1970s.
4. J&M RECORDING, New Orleans, 1940s-1950s.
5. THE MEMPHIS RECORDING SERVICE, Memphis, 1950s.
6. FAME RECORDING, Muscle Shoals, Alabama, 1960s-1970s.
7. THE MUSCLE SHOALS SOUND STUDIOS, Sheffield, Ala., 1960s-1970s.
8. SIGMA SOUND, Philadelphia, 1960s-1970s.
9. UNITED RECORDING, Los Angeles, 1960s-1970s.
10. WESTERN RECORDERS, Los Angeles, 1960s-1970s.
11. ATLANTIC RECORDS STUDIO, New York, 1960s-1970s.
12. KING RECORDING STUDIOS, Cincinnati, 1950s-1960s.
13. WOODLAND SOUND STUDIOS, Nashville, 1960s-1970s.

*With apologies to many other deserving studios. The numerical listing is for convenience; the studios have no particular ranking of importance. They also contributed to the national music business.

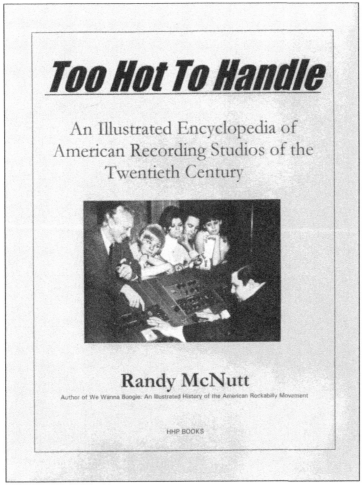

About the Author

In the 1970s, award-winning freelance writer Randy McNutt started producing records in Cincinnati with singer-songwriter Wayne Perry. His recordings have appeared on a dozen independent labels in Europe and the United States. He has worked as a reporter for *The Cincinnati Enquirer*, a contributing editor for several magazines, and a staff writer for *Design*. His books include *We Wanna Boogie: An Illustrated History of the American Rockabilly Movement* and *Too Hot to Handle: An Illustrated Encyclopedia of American Recording Studios of the Twentieth Century*. He writes about the old record business and its performers at homeofthehits.blogspot.com. He continues to record on magnetic tape.

Randy McNutt at the console in Studio B, Hamilton, Ohio, 1974.
The recorder is an eight-track Ampex.

REWIND

Made in United States
North Haven, CT
07 May 2024

52032019R00128